D1572522

SAINT WITH A GUN
The Unlawful American Private Eye

SAINT WITH A GUN
The Unlawful American Private Eye

William Ruehlmann

New York: NEW YORK UNIVERSITY PRESS

1974

Mike Barry.
   Permission to quote from *Bay Prowler* by Mike Barry, copyright © 1973 by
Mike Barry, is granted by Berkley Publishing Corporation and Robert P. Mills,
156 East 52nd St., New York, New York 10022.
Raymond Chandler.
   Grateful acknowledgment is extended to Alfred A. Knopf, Inc., Hamish Hamil-
ton Ltd., and Raymond Chandler's Estate for permission to quote from the follow-
ing copyrighted works: *The Big Sleep, Farewell, My Lovely,* and *The Lady in the
Lake* by Raymond Chandler.
   Permission to quote from *The Little Sister* by Raymond Chandler, copyright
© 1949 by Raymond Chandler, is granted by the Houghton Mifflin Company,
Hamish Hamilton Ltd., and Raymond Chandler's Estate.
John Evans.
   Permission to quote from *Halo in Blood* by John Evans, copyright © 1946 by
The Bobbs-Merrill Company, is granted by Howard Browne.
Ron Goulart.
   Permission to quote from *The Hardboiled Dicks: An Anthology of Pulp Detec-
tive Fiction,* edited by Ron Goulart, copyright © 1965 by Ron Goulart, is granted
by Sherbourne Press.
Brett Halliday.
   Permission to quote from *Dividend on Death* by Brett Halliday, copyright ©
1939 by Henry Holt and Company, Inc., is granted by Davis Dresser.
Dashiell Hammett.
   Grateful acknowledgment is extended to Random House, Inc. and The Harold
Matson Company, Inc. for permission to quote from the following copyrighted
work: *The Big Knockover: Selected Stories and Short Novels of Dashiell Hammett,*
edited by Lillian Hellman, copyright © 1962, 1965, 1966 by Lillian Hellman.
Copyright © 1924, 1925, 1926, 1927, 1929 by Pro-Distributors Company, Inc. Copy-
right renewed 1951–54 and 1956 by Popular Publications, Inc. Assigned to Lillian
Hellman as Successor to Dashiell Hammett.
   Grateful acknowledgment is extended to Alfred A. Knopf, Inc. for permission
to quote from the following copyrighted works: *Red Harvest* and *The Maltese
Falcon* by Dashiell Hammett.
James Jones.
   Permission to quote from *A Touch of Danger* by James Jones, copyright © 1973
by James Jones, is granted by Doubleday and Company, Inc.
Henry Kane.
   Permission to quote from *Armchair in Hell* by Henry Kane, copyright © 1948
by Henry Kane, is granted by Henry Kane.
Ross Macdonald.
   Grateful acknowledgment is extended to Kenneth Millar for permission to quote
from *The Galton Case* by Ross Macdonald, copyright © 1959 by Ross Macdonald,
Sleeping Beauty by Ross Macdonald, copyright © 1973 by Ross Macdonald, and
The Underground Man by Ross Macdonald, copyright © 1971 by Ross Macdonald.
Peter McCurtin.
   Permission to quote from *Manhattan Massacre* by Peter McCurtin, copyright
© 1973 by Lorelei Publications, Inc., is granted by co-publishers Lorelei Publica-
tions, Inc. and Dell Publishing Company, Inc.

To Lynn
whose giving hand never held a gun

Foreword

At our beginnings as a nation the Founding Fathers ruled out cruel and unusual punishments and never since have we, as a people, been comfortable with our system of justice. Crime in general and violent crime in particular is still with us; and, in our rage against today's violence, all too few of us can be convinced that we are afflicted with no more of it in our own time than was the citizenry of those earlier days when cruel and unusual punishments were imposed, or even than the society of those still earlier days when cruel punishments were so common that they had not yet become unusual.

We tend to be impatient and resentful of the presumption of innocence, of the rules of evidence, of protection of the rights of the accused. We are confused about the purposes of our criminal justice system and we find it frustratingly ineffective. Crime and violence are all around us and nothing is being done about it that we can find emotionally satisfying.

The complaints are familiar. The rights of the accused? Did he consider the rights of his victims? Imprisonment? What good is that? Pamper him in jail and after a few years turn him loose on parole and he's on the streets again to molest us. The punishment doesn't fit the crime. We don't get even with the criminals. That "even" of "getting even" will, furthermore, seem equitable only under a usurer's definition of equity. Make him suffer and not only as he made his victims suffer but with heavy interest.

The arguments are also familiar. If light punishment won't change the criminal, then heavier punishment will and always heavier all the way through to the *reductio ad absurdum* of destroying him to save him. The arguments, however, are only rationalizations of a gut need, the emotional demand for revenge.

ix

William Ruehlmann's perceptive examination of the heroes of American Private-Eye fiction reveals them for what they are: detectives only in part, if at all, but almost invariably avengers. The loners of the Old West who took justice into their own hands (because presumably out in the wild country there was no place else for it to repose), now appear as the loners of the corrupt cities and they are represented as taking justice into their own hands because the legal machinery is not providing satisfactory vengeance.

I am reminded of a luncheon party at an American general's table in North Africa during World War II. The general had a guest, Andre Gide. Also at table that day was a high-ranking OSS executive. (For those who may not know or who have forgotten it began as OSS. Alphabetical metamorphosis later made it CIA.) The OSS man undertook to lead the table talk into areas that might be congenial to France's famous man of letters. He asked Gide for his opinion of American novelists. Gide told him that there was only one worthy of serious consideration and that one was Dashiell Hammett because, Gide explained, Hammett was the only American novelist who kept his work free of the pollution of moral judgments.

It is more than possible that this was not Andre Gide's most seriously considered opinion. One must take into account the likelihood that, confronted with a coterie of General-Staff types, not to speak of a general whose preferred reading was Westerns, Gide found irresistable the opportunity to drop a critical bombshell. The virtue he attributed to Hammett, however, is there. Hammett took the crime novel out of the polite milieu it had come to inhabit and set it firmly in its natural habitat, a corrupt and violent society. His Private Eyes were men with the competence to survive in that habitat. They waged no crusades. They pretended to no nobility. They did what was necessary for survival and they did it with skill and toughness. They also did it without self-deception. They survived but they knew themselves to have been corrupted in the process, and they knew that it was the corruption of getting even.

Dashiell Hammett's imitators and successors in the Private-Eye story have not imitated him in this one respect which won him the Gide accolade. They do make moral judgments. If the best of them invest their avenging heroes with some rueful realization that they are themselves being corrupted by their acts of violence, they nevertheless make their heroes men with a mission, men who, because of their devotion to the good cause, choose to pay the price of their own corruption.

The worst of these writers, however (and among them are those who ring up the highest sales figures), plough only those Hammett furrows that produce the greatest royalty yield. Their Private Eyes are the stern moralists who permit no wrong to go unrequited. Each painful death is overmatched with a death more painful. Each sadism is topped with a sadism more vile, and all these retributive acts are presented as further ennobling the right-eous avenger. He tortures and he kills, but because his cause is just, the end doesn't do anything so piddling as merely to justify the means. It endows the means with every virtue. Was St. George reduced in stature by his killing of the dragon?

If you should ask the writers of the Private-Eye stories about what they do, their answers may be as various as their number is great but there will be one common element. Whatever their pretentions or lack of pretention, they will all be agreed that they give the public what the public wants.

William Ruehlmann has done a penetrating analysis of just what it is that this public wants and has come to interesting and chilling conclusions about what the want indicates of the character of that huge public.

If I were to take issue with anything in his argument, it is that he has limited himself in his consideration of the American Pri-vate-Eye hero only to the Private Eye as he reveals something about his American readers. I should like to add to his observa-tions the thought that these American Private-Eye stories are an export commodity. Their great sales are not limited to the home market. Their foreign sales are also massive.

We might in humility think that foreigners read them to feed their contempt for our lawlessness, but one might well take a close look at that contempt. There is more than a little awe in it and more than a little envy. We are not alone. Most of what we call the civilized world is with us in this frustration of having given up at least ostensibly a justice that is synonymous with revenge.

In reading our novels foreigners have long tended to see us as a people who, having space around us, could enjoy the luxury of living with elbows not neatly tucked in and free of the need to trim the edges off our individual liberties lest we infringe on the liberty of a neighbor. In talking books with European friends, I frequently find myself much their inferior in knowledge of the works of James Fenimore Cooper. From Cooper they form their admiring impressions of how we began and of what we are—free men in the wilderness who improvise our law, our justice, and our morality as we ride along. The phrase has fallen from fashion but the concept is still alive: "Nature's noblemen."

People abroad also move west with our wilderness-men heroes and are as much the fans of the shootout as is any American. I am remembering an afternoon at Fontenoy. The abbey ruin is on private property and only a farmyard separates the medieval remains from the home of the proprietor. I was poking about the ruins in a driving rain when suddenly it cleared and, as quickly as the sun broke out of the clouds, a small boy burst out of the house across the yard. As he came through the door, he drew, whipping the two six-shooters out of the twin holsters of his Western gunbelt. He was obviously the fastest gun of the Cote d'Or. If in Bavaria the Leatherstocking is as familiar as the *Lederhosen*, the shoot-'em-up buckaroos gallop from kill to kill in Burgundy, Buckinghamshire, and the Bernese Oberland.

It may be that it is not a national malady but a broader malaise of this our Age of Reason, a universal itch to take justice into our own hands, to give as good as we get (if not better), to let us good guys have a share in the intoxicating joys of sadism. Why should the criminals have all the fun and we, the pure in heart, have none?

Aaron Marc Stein

Introduction

When he shot George Wallace of Alabama four times point blank with a snub-nosed .38, pale Arthur Bremer wore a red, white, and blue shirt and a tight smile. His math teacher remembered him as being well-groomed; the mother of his girl friend recalled his courtesy.

Lieutenant William Calley prayed by his bunk to be a good soldier the night before he lined up the villagers of Mylai 4 in an irrigation ditch and gave his men the order to "waste" them.

Charles "Tex" Watson had been the six-foot two-inch, one hundred ninety-pound former All District halfback for the Farmersville high school football team. Later he acquired a nine-shot, walnut-handled, fifteen-inch blue steel revolver that fired .22-calibre long rifle bullets, a bayonet, and a body count of his own at the Sharon Tate killings in sunny cliffside California.

One deservedly much-decorated Air Force general flew seventy-six successful missions in World War II and sustained a continuing record of concern for the welfare of his men. After he had taken command of all U.S. air units in Vietnam and determined the war was not going as he wanted it, John Lavelle unleashed for four months a legion of F-4 Phantom jets on unauthorized targets of his own choosing and falsified the reports after.

These individuals and others offered a new slant on American good and American evil. For they had been cast as heroes from the start: Bremer, the blond-haired inoffensive around-the-block Anykid who lifted weights and read books; Calley, green but gutsy, the eager and committed combat soldier played so often in the past by actors like Van Johnson, all freckles and teeth; Watson, another beamish boy right off the Wheaties box; and Lavelle, the well-seasoned warrior with a wall of war ribbons and a John Wayne jaw. All were loners moving like romantic Chosen in an unromantic world; they marched to solipsismal battle hymns while earthly matters marked time. Their significance for the seventies was clearly that the real enemies were emerging in unexpected attitudes: everybody had been armed for years against either the Russians or some snaggletoothed wild-haired anarchist dope freak, and along came clean-cut anthem-intoning messiahs with mild eyes and a sense of mission more dangerous. These men bore the image of the FBI agent, not the public enemy. And then even the FBI itself came under stunned scrutiny when Patrick Gray burned obvious evidence among his Christmas trash. The implications of insular conviction became graver than those of ideological antagonism, explaining at once an administration's involvement in Watergate and a nation's in Vietnam. Something was the matter with America, and it resided in the terrible duality of its heroes. The zeal of William Calley is celebrated in Samson and abhorred in Eichmann; the dawn patrols of John Lavelle are marked alike with distinguished courage and unmitigated madness.

The beginning of this book probably came when I met an American hero in Tucson. He was an ex-Marine who collected fundamentalist literature and spoke of missions for Christ; he had whole files of unofficial, personal investigations on people and had even Scotch-taped J. Edgar Hoover's picture over his desk. He was quite certain the Judgment was at hand, and he was its instrument. He always carried a loaded gun, working alone and without pay. He had his crusade: he would kill evil.

Later in Cincinnati a pornographic bookstore opened in the suburbs. A priest told me he wanted to take photographs of the patrons at the door to shame them into staying out. He did not know how the pictures might be used, but like the Marine he believed they were evidence. Later the bookstore closed down, not because of the picketers nor in response to the outcry of enraged citizens' committees, but because someone had been shooting out the windows with a carbine.

In the same city I testified for the defense in an obscenity suit against another bookstore, arguing that the state's exhibits could not be considered incongruent with the community standard in materials available at any newsstand or drug store. The judge freely admitted off the record that he had determined his verdict long before I had been called to the stand. In court he affirmed he was more qualified to judge the community standard than I was and refused to admit my testimony about it. When I testified instead that the materials in question were defensible as art and literature, the prosecutor asked me if I wanted a diseased mind consulting them for medical help; then he asked me if I wanted my niece, who is eight, to pose for explicit photographs. What bothered me was not these strange questions but the fact that the judge had at once taken down my name and address in careful longhand.

The armed man who kept files in Tucson and the priest who believed in moral suasion in Cincinnati shared visions with the common pleas judge who required no testimony to arrive at the truth. Each saw himself on the side of the angels and no sense of impurity nor motive of personal gain stained his cause. Each was a responsible member of the community, or thought he was. Each subscribed to a Higher Law that governed the affairs of men, and each believed his role to be earthly arbiter of that Law. The result was that the best men were capable of the worst crimes for the best reasons: the armed man was capable of murder; the priest was capable of the abrogation of individual rights; and the judge was capable of subverting the judicial system he served. The anonymous marksman who shot out the windows of that suburban bookstore was without doubt acting on a conviction that he was saving the community from sin; if anybody inside was killed in the process, he had it coming. It was, after all, open season on devils.

That notion is not one exclusive to the right wing. The instinctive enemies of George Wallace have always been the intellectuals, and my memory of their reaction to the shooting on U.S. 1 is ugly. The morning after in an English Department mail room, before word was out on the gutshot governor's possible paralysis, professors exchanged opinions not distinguished for their humanity. "If you're going to pull an assassination," somebody said, "you ought to do it properly"; "He had it coming," said somebody else. That phrase again, and from the upper ranks of a university, where liberal arts often means learning which things to weep for. It is a reflection evidently foreign to a lot of people that *nobody* has it coming, nobody at all.

So this book began to happen when matters of heroic ambivalence struck home. How to account for a Lavelle, who performed alone and bravely for his nation and slew thousands for a conviction? Or for a moralist President elected on a law and order platform but responsible for a campaign linked to libel and burglary? Or for an entire military offensive conducted in Cambodia without the knowledge of the country it represented? The answer seemed to reside somewhere in the American vision of personal destiny, a vision most manifest in our popular fiction.

The private eye is the most modern of American heroes, and he has long been emblem for that same mad Hyde sunk beneath a surface Jack Armstrong Jekyll. He carries memories of Bogart in a trenchcoat, solitary, laconic, a cigarette canted down from the corner of the mouth. Disaffiliated Bill Hart gone urban, he moves among the runs and alleys of the American metropolis with a real awareness of what an unclean region it is. He is at his best in situations calling for physical courage, facing down even the big shots of both gang and government. But he is at his worst in moments of meditation, pursuing the terrible implications of his drive for rough justice. In *The Big Sleep,* a Howard Hawks film that retains the spirit if not the letter of Raymond Chandler's novel, gunmen wait in ambush beyond the door, but Bogart encourages a gangster to go through in his stead by pinking him once or twice with a .45. It is a calculated execution that will consistently be reenacted in private eye literature. Ironically, Bogart had the credentials; he became famous playing hoods, not heroes. But the private eye, half saint and half headsman, remains a hero to his readers and a moral horror to his critics. His contradictory personality is a reflection of the American heroic dilemma; the private eye is Lavelle deplaned, and I believe the literature that is his record reveals things about him and about us.

Acknowledgments

I extend my personal thanks to Arlene Elder, William God-shalk, and Wayne Miller of the University of Cincinnati for their patient readings of this book in manuscript and for their many useful suggestions for its improvement.

Contents

"I'll be judge, I'll be jury," said cunning old Fury;
"I'll try the whole cause and condemn you to death."
                                —*Alice in Wonderland*

ONE. The Clergy of the Damned

"It is the weapon in our own hands that finally destroys us."
—Uncle Abner

In a novel published not long ago by Mickey Spillane, one of the characters stands over another and muses:

> Just how *did* you kill a dragon? I could bury the ax in his belly. That would be fun, all right. Stick it right in the middle of his skull and it would look a lot better. They wouldn't come fooling around after seeing pictures of that. How about the neck? One whack and his head would roll like the Japs used to do. But nuts, why be that kind?
> This guy was *really* going to die.[1]

What is interesting about the passage is not that the narrator is an evident psychopath, but that he is the hero. In him is invested the moral sanction of his fictive world. If a substantial portion of the American reading public responds positively to such a hero, the fact is not without significance; and Spillane's books at last count had sold more than fifty-five million copies, most of them in the United States.

An age is revealed by its fantasies; Spillane reveals something about ours. For popular culture is history in caricature, an exaggerated portrait of a nation's psychic nature, and the urban murder story is, and has been, the American waking nightmare of its own civic reality.

The private eye is at the center of the urban murder story and is substantially a creation of the American imagination. His authentic existence is a long way from the vision of Mickey Spillane; legislation in New York, for example, neither permits the private eye to carry a badge nor even call himself a private detective. In the unlikely event that he should carry a gun, he must have a permit for it like anyone else. And he operates under severe restrictions:

> Under state regulations, the prospective private eye must have been regularly employed for more than three years as

3

a police detective, a sheriff, an agent of one of the Federal investigative agencies or a member of a city police department with a rank higher than a patrolman. He must pass a written examination, meet the standards of a rigid character check and be able to show that he has never been convicted of a felony or of such misdemeanors as "unlawful entry of a building. . . ." [2]

Further, the nature of his duties is codified under a license that can be withdrawn by the state upon violation.

> What he is empowered to do is to protect person and property; to inquire into crimes; to investigate the causes of accidents and fires; to check the character of employes and trial witnesses; to examine the financial responsibilities of businesses and insurance applicants, and to search for missing persons. In none of these functions, though, may he make an arrest or break existing laws. [3]

He tends to behave himself because of the restrictions placed upon him. He does not make much money. In the main he is an innocuous figure unassociated with personal heroism and connected more closely with tedium than with romance. Or even pathos: George V. Higgins, writer (*The Friends of Eddie Coyle*, 1972) and assistant district attorney, observes that

> the Private Investigator excels at catching wayward spouses *in flagrante delicto* at casual motels. In a serious case he is an out-and-out horror; the only one I ever saw, close up, in a significant matter was charged as the defendant in a case alleging illegal possession of a machine gun. He wept. [4]

The private eye of fiction is, then, an invention; only a literary heraldry can account for him.

He belongs to the detective story genre, which was invented by an American, but the major influences on it were English until the 1920s. Even then it was evidence for cultural identity; certainly Victorian England found an archetype in Sherlock Holmes. The Great Detective's "science of deduction" (actually induction as he practiced it) was an expression of the era's faith in empiricism as evidenced by Darwin and Huxley, while his affinity for cocaine and the violin was rooted in values of the aesthetic movement which degenerated from Pater to Wilde. The moralism of the day left Watson the soul of sexual reticence and Holmes a misogynist. Conan Doyle's evocation of the London underworld was surrealism for gentlemen, an afforded sense of evil stirring among the sinews under that staunch nineteenth-century skin. The ultimate horror in the Holmes stories sprang from biology amok—the poisonous jellyfish in "The Adventure of the Lion's Mane" (1926), the swamp adder in "The Speckled Band" (1892), the gigantic mastiff in *The Hound of the Baskervilles* (1902)— something reason could handle: a prenuclear, premutational self-possession.

America transformed the detective hero by supplying him with the accouterments of an ethnic past. The private eye novel was a Western that took place somewhere else. The eye traced his lineage back through the novels of Zane Grey and Owen Wister's *Virginian* (1902) to the frontier romances of James Fenimore Cooper. "Men murdered themselves into this democracy," [5] D. H. Lawrence wrote in his essay on Cooper's Leatherstocking stories and went on to delineate the terrible duality of the prototypical American hero, Natty Bumppo:

He is a moralizer, but he always tries to moralize from actual experiences, not from theory. He says: "Hurt nothing unless you're forced to." Yet he gets his deepest thrill of gratification, perhaps, when he puts a bullet through the heart of a beautiful buck, as it stoops to drink at the lake. Or when he brings the invisible bird fluttering down in death, out of the high blue. "Hurt nothing unless you're forced to." And yet he lives by death, by killing the wild things of the air and earth.[6]

The Natty Bumppo who flees the sound of the ax is one with the Hawkeye who trembles in his eagerness to get a shot off at an enemy.[7] If Natty is "one who keeps his moral integrity hard and intact," [8] there are ambiguities in that integrity that have lingered from the literature of Cooper's time to that of our own.

The American Western is a morality play whose end is retribu-

tion, not redemption. Jack Schaefer's *Shane* (1949) is the essence
of the myth that the gunfighter does not triumph over evil, he
merely survives it. The sodbusters may settle on the bodies of the
enemies he has killed for them, but his sins leave him no place
among them, hopelessly excluded like Moses from the Promised
Land. Behind him remains a memory in the mind of a small boy
who sees Shane's "beauty" in his ability to perform.

> I would think of him in each of the moments that revealed
> him to me. I would think of him most vividly in that single
> flashing instant when he whirled to shoot Fletcher on the
> balcony at Grafton's saloon. I would see again the power and
> grace of a coordinate force beautiful beyond comprehension.
> I would see the man and the weapon wedded in one invisible
> deadliness. I would see the man and the tool, a good man and
> a good tool, doing what had to be done.[9]

"What had to be done" was provoked murder. But it was murder
done in the name of the nesters, not in the name of the cattlemen;
that it was therefore just is in the best traditions of frontier juris-
prudence. "It did not matter," writes historian Joe B. Frantz,
"that you killed, so much as whom you killed." [10]

In the American West, "the lawman was as closely associated
with violence as the outlaw." [11] Wyatt Earp and Wild Bill Hickok
were more often in open competition with the side of the law
than on it; and Judge Roy Bean, "The Law West of the Pecos,"
was less an officer of the court than its enemy. This moral muddi-
ness indigenous to the Western became by birthright a quality of
the Eastern—or private eye novel. If Raymond Chandler early
saw the detective as "a man of honor . . . by instinct, by inevita-
bility, without thought of it, and certainly without saying it," [12]
The Times Literary Supplement later insisted "the modern private investigator hero is all too often a sadistic, alcoholic philan-
derer whose behavior is worse than that of the criminals he is
opposing." [13]

The reason for the American response to Mickey Spillane cannot reside in the commonly offered reasons for reading detective
fiction because private eye fiction is not precisely the same. G. K.
Chesterton saw the detective story as "only a game; and in that

game the reader is not only wrestling with the criminal but with the author." [14] Dorothy Sayers suggested that "man, not satisfied with the mental confusion and unhappiness to be derived from contemplating the cruelties of life and the riddle of the universe, delights to occupy his leisure moments with puzzles and buga-boos." [15] These may be reasons for reading about Father Brown and Lord Peter Wimsey, but they are not reasons for reading about Mike Hammer and John Shaft. In his typically acrimonious essay "Who Cares Who Killed Roger Ackroyd?" Edmund Wilson comes closer to the American reader's motivation: what Raymond Chandler writes "is not simply a question . . . of a puzzle which has been put together but of a malaise conveyed to the reader, the horror of a hidden conspiracy that is continually turning up in the most varied and unlikely forms." [16] In "Why Do People Read Detective Stories?" Wilson ponders further. If these stories are not games, then they sustain a literary need different from the human need for conundrums; perhaps they serve the human need for the solutions to them.

> The detective story has kept its hold; had even, in the two decades between the great wars, become more popular than ever before; and there is, I believe, a deep reason for this. The world during those years was ridden by an all-pervasive feeling of guilt and by a fear of impending disaster which it seemed hopeless to try to avert because it never seemed conclusively possible to pin down the responsibility. . . . [T]he supercilious and omniscient detective . . . knows exactly where to fix the guilt. [17]

The suspicion that the detective story is a purgative for guilt was shared by W. H. Auden: "the typical reader of detective stories is, like myself, a person who suffers from a sense of sin." [18] Thus, "the fantasy . . . which the detective story addict indulges in is the fantasy of being restored to the Garden of Eden, to a state of innocence, where he may know love as love and law as law." [19] The idea of law is important in the detective novel; it provides the framework under which the guilty are punished and the innocent vindicated. But law is variously defined in the private eye novel of this country. Our separate perception becomes clearer

in another essay by Chesterton in which he defines the legal substance of the detective: "those who have enjoyed the *roman
policier* must have noted one thing, that when the murderer is
caught he is hardly ever hanged. 'That,' says Sherlock Holmes, 'is
the advantage of being a private detective'; after he has caught
he can set free." [20]

This would be scanned. The English detective may indeed set
free—Sherlock Holmes certainly did so on more than one occasion
—but the American private eye punishes. Like Herman Melville's
Captain Vere, it is not sufficient for him to isolate guilt; he must
also deal with it, and in doing so he loses any prior claim to innocence. The idea of meting out punishment for sin—assigning the
scarlet letter—is peculiarly American and manifest in the private eye novel. Historian David Abrahamsen reports that "the
Puritan's use of force . . . has influenced our present national
attitude"; [21] it is no accident that Mickey Spillane is a lapsed Jeho-
vah's Witness, and his apocalyptic moralism finds expression in
mythic tales of God's enforcers.

In a thoughtful dissertation on the private eye as violent hero,
Robert Brown Parker argues that the detective's

> triumph is not a triumph of toughness, but of virtue, inno-
> cence, which, in the world of the private eye only the tough
> can sustain. For the private eye is a catalyst. His story is the
> interaction of his innocence with the pervasive corruption of
> his society. The society is not reformed, but the hero is not
> corrupted. [22]

This has been the standard view. But the typical tough-guy private eye does not merely interact with social corruption, he col-
laborates in it. The society is certainly not reformed, but the hero
is corrupted—through the well-intentioned yet dangerous application of his self-justifying moralism. As former Attorney General
John Mitchell cautioned with unintentional irony, "Don't mark
what we say—watch what we do." While the private eye speaks of
evenhanded justice, he performs violence not only on the mis-
creant but on the American legal system as well. His story is not
one of juridical equity but of personal vengeance. In Dashiell
Hammett's landmark *Red Harvest* (1929), the Continental Op

typically ends his blood odyssey "trying to fix up my reports so that they would not read as if I had broken as many Agency rules, state laws and human bones as I had." [23] If, like Gatsby, he is committed "to the following of a grail," [24] like Gatsby—and indeed like Gatsby's flawed predecessor Lancelot—he is an ill-made knight not good enough for the job. Impartiality eludes him. His sometime sensitivity to the nature of the human consequences of his actions condemns rather than redeems him.

The fact is that private eye novels are vigilante literature, and their peculiar appeal lies in reader identification with a hero whose brutality avenges not only fictional transgression but American urban frustration as well. In *The Six-Gun Mystique* (1973) popular culturist John G. Cawelti acknowledges that "formula stories seem to be one way in which the individuals in a culture act out certain unconscious or repressed needs, or express in an overt and symbolic fashion certain latent motives which they must give expression to, but cannot face openly." [25] The private detective who not only tracks down his quarry but executes him too is reenacting the American retributive morality; the eye's city is Salem Again where ritual deaths expiate our helplessness in more real regions. Richard Maxwell Brown reported the following to the National Commission on the Causes and Prevention of Violence at the end of the last decade:

> Most urban Americans, particularly in the largest cities, are firm in their belief that there is too much crime, that their persons or property are in danger, and that regular law enforcement is not coping with the problem. The same feelings in earlier times led Americans to resort to vigilantism. [26]

Richard Hofstadter argues further that "lynching and vigilantism have so few parallels or equivalents elsewhere that they can be regarded as a distinctly American institution." [27] The eye, above the underworld and the law alike, superior to the stupid cops, makes straight the way of the Lord in the tradition of Bible Belt revivalism. "In his own sweet way," writes George V. Higgins, "the Private Investigator is a straight guy's one-man Mob, an alternative system of law enforcement." [28]

The private eye has been perceived by critics as astute as Leslie

Fiedler to be "the embodiment of innocence moving untouched through universal guilt," [29] but his innocence is the innocence of the psychopath, not the saint. His qualities of toughness and physical courage have perhaps blinded the hasty reader into some false admiration for a figure who is, in sum, indistinguishable in method from his adversaries. Raphael Patai has written of the compelling impetus of myth:

> [The superiority of the hero] is so impressive that the cause he represents becomes automatically right and our total sympathy is immediately captured by him, just as there could be no question that Herakles was right and the hundreds of antagonists whom he killed in various ways were wrong, and, being wrong, deserved to die.
>
> Here, precisely, lies the psychological significance of the Herakles myth and its heirs, the hero serials. They enable us, in fact compel us, not only to identify with their heroes, but to derive deep emotional-moral satisfaction from the feats that they (and through them, we) perform.[30]

But the response to these stories would not have been quite so overwhelming without the collaboration of American sympathy for retributive justice and impatience with due process, and these are the reasons for the unparalleled popularity of Mickey Spillane.

The vindication of a vengeful God has long been the American detective's appointed task. In Melville Davisson Post's distant and seminal "Doomdorf Mystery" (1911), sage colonial sleuth Uncle Abner, "the right hand of the land" (p. 263),[31] sets out in pursuit of a Virginia bootlegger. "The work of this brew, which had the odors of Eden and the impulses of the devil in it," the narrator explains, "could be borne no longer." When the bootlegger is discovered dead by gunshot on their arrival, Abner's associate, Squire Randolph, would seek out the murderer; but Abner maintains "we are in God's court" (p. 267) and that the bootlegger has been taken off by His "curse" (p. 273). Thus a sunray's magnified heat through a window is shown to have set off the fowling piece that killed old Doomdorf. "It is fire from heaven!" proclaims Abner, in a world "filled with the mysterious justice of God!" (p. 274).

If God is a tad rough on brewers, that is only as it should be. (American awe for higher law and contempt for the earthly may as well explain Prohibition's inception and the subsequent whole-sale disregard for it.) It is Abner's nephew who aptly observes: "My uncle belonged to the church militant, and his God was a war-god." [32] That justification hangs behind the Spillane ethos which, in 1973, can draw careful distinction between "murder" (public nuisance) and "killing" (public service).

Mike Hammer, the private eye at his least evasive, is clearly a vigilante in conception and execution. Christopher LaFarge sees him as the "apotheosis of McCarthyism": "the destruction of evil persons or at least of those that Hammer decides are evil . . . justifies the means to that end." [33] "The Hammer character," writes Archie H. Jones, "clearly reveals the Puritan strain in the hero myth. He believes in individual responsibility not just for oneself but for the whole society; he assumes that all men (except in practice himself) are irretrievably sinful; and he is willing, indeed eager, to believe that his will is the will of God." [34] John G. Cawelti is perhaps too reassuring in his comment that Hammer is "a prophet of the past," "a final outcry of the evangelistic sub-culture of rural America"; [35] rather Hammer, inseparable from a tradition that continues, may serve as prophet for the future as well. He was born in the American admiration for instant and admonitory action in figures like Washington Irving's Brom Bones, sustained and enlarged in Cooper, and given a modern milieu in the semi-nonfictional works of Allan Pinkerton. He grew under the hands of that school of writers which came to be called "hard-boiled" in pulps like *Black Mask* in the 1920s and 1930s, emerging out of a time when the frontier was finished and the back alleys of America were becoming the loci for motorized badmen warring over the kind of water rights that came out of a keg. Dashiell Hammett's Sam Spade, Raymond Chandler's Philip Marlowe, and Ross Macdonald's Lew Archer supplied him form; but now he has moved even beyond Spillane in books that remove from him all legal sanction and reduce him to a private citizen berserk—which is only reflective of the world beyond the novels. Joe B. Frantz identifies the dangers evident in a social sys-tem still harboring a cowboy mythos:

The difficulty with frontier vigilantism is that it has no stopping place. Men accustomed to taking law into their hands continue to take law into their hands even after regular judicial processes are constituted. They continue to take the law into their hands right into these days of the 1960's. They do not approve of a man or a situation, and they cannot wait for the regular process to assist their realization. They are not aware of the extension of the frontier spirit down to themselves. But they do know that they must get rid of the offending member or section of civilization. So they burn down a ghetto, they loot and pillage, they bury three civil rights workers beneath a dam, or they shoot a man in a caravan in Dallas or on a motel balcony in Memphis.[36]

Indeed, in the words of John Seelye, "the Indian Hater has outlived his quarry." [37]

"Tell me what murders are committed and what is done about them," writes psychologist Fredric Wertham, "and I'll tell you what society you live in." [38] In recent popular fiction the private eye has become the emblem of public rage directed against problems without solutions. Writing of Hammer, Russel Nye in his popular arts study *The Unembarrassed Muse* (1970) claims that "he offers a simple, direct answer to some of society's more frustrating problems—the Mafia, crooked cops, big graft, foreign spies, gangsters, and the like. In other words, he gets results." [39] The stylized vendettas of Spillane's successors are assaults upon a reality the American at large feels powerless to control—a reality in which the government and the Mafia do not materially differ. Lieutenant William Calley's testimony at his trial for murder in Mylai might have been the testimony of Mike Hammer; even more disturbingly, so might that of White House adviser John Ehrlichman at the hearings on the Watergate.

Donald E. Westlake's *Cops and Robbers* (1972) is a novel (and later a film) about this reversal of roles; the good guys are harder to distinguish when police officers become stick-up men. But they become stick-up men for real reasons that involve the entropic urban swarm around them. Westlake recounts the outburst of one cracking citizen as he climbs from a manhole after a subway breakdown:

"This city is a disgrace! It's a disgrace! You aren't safe here! And who cares? Does anybody care? Everything breaks down, and nobody gives a God damn! Everybody's in the *union!* Teachers on strike, subways on strike, cops on strike, sanitation on strike. Money money money, and when they work do they *do* anything? Do they teach? Don't make me laugh! The subways are a menace, they're a menace! Sanitation? Look at the streets! Big raises, big pay, and look at the streets! And you *cops!* Gimme gimme gimme, and where are you? Your apartment gets robbed, and where *are* you? Some dope addict attacks your wife in the street, and where's the *cops?*" (p. 36) [40]

The sense of vulnerability in any citizen springs as well from his sense of no recourse—the telephone company can't be petitioned, it's a monopoly; the incoming bills are wrong, but the computer can't be convinced; the parking ticket is irrevocable, and so is the supremacy of the mobster. Westlake draws a scene in which Anthony Vigano, racketeer, leaves the squadroom after precinct questioning. The cops escort him out.

Nobody said a word all the way down in the car, but now, once we were in the elevator and headed up for the fourth floor, Charles Reddy suddenly said, "You don't seem worried, Tony."

Vigano gave him a casual glance. If it bugged him to be called by his first name he didn't show it. He said, "Worried? I could buy and sell you, what's to worry? I'll be home with my family tonight, and four years from now when the case is over in the courts I won't lose." (p. 46)

As this inverted world fastens itself upon the deadening senses of an ash-inhaling populace, the result is, as Westlake demonstrates, the same as it would be in any overcrowded Skinner box: "We all of us get together in that city like hungry animals jammed in together in a pit, and we beat on each other because that's all we know how to do, and after a while all of us have turned ourselves into people you don't want to bring your kids up among" (p. 53). Into this social stew moves the fictive private eye, The

Expediter, anodyne for the outrage of the millions. Through him the mail goes through, the red tape is cut, the recalcitrant repairman is blown to jelly on the spot.

In 1942 Nicholas Blake (pseudonym of C. Day-Lewis) could write that the detective was "the Fairy Godmother of the twentieth century folk-myth"; [41] Blake was English. If the modern American version is less fairy godmother than Demon Godfather, it is because he has always borne a distinct resemblance to the Brando role. The private eye novel from its inception has offered up a vision of rampant and inescapable corruption moving beyond the margins of control; it has always sustained the suspicion that institutions set up to save society are destroying it; and its assumption has ever been that justice is best served by unjust methods.

Between the eye's conception and his performance is the key to the American heroic dilemma. Raymond Chandler began his first novel, *The Big Sleep* (1939), with Philip Marlowe's view of a mural in a hallway:

> Over the entrance doors, which would have let in a troop of Indian elephants, there was a broad stained-glass panel showing a knight in dark armor rescuing a lady who was tied to a tree and didn't have any clothes on but some very long and convenient hair. The knight had pushed the visor of his helmet back to be sociable, and he was fiddling with the knots on the ropes that tied the lady to the tree and not getting anywhere. I stood there and thought that if I lived in the house, I would sooner or later have to climb up there and help him. [42]

That harmless wish could turn into an obsession, and dwindling possibilities for a romantic's emotional survival can manifest themselves in spiritual D.T.'s. It was not long after his wife's death that La Jolla police discovered a laughing Chandler seated in a shower stall shooting high-caliber holes in the ceiling. [43]

NOTES

1. Mickey Spillane, *The Girl Hunters* (New York: Dutton, 1962), p. 206.

2. Thomas Meehan, "The Case of the Private Eye," *The New York Times Magazine,* November 15, 1959, p. 34.

3. Meehan, p. 34.

4. George V. Higgins, "The Private Eye as Illegal Hero," *Esquire,* December 1972, p. 351.

5. D. H. Lawrence, "Fenimore Cooper's Leatherstocking Novels," in *Studies in Classic American Literature* (1923; rpt. Garden City, N.Y.: Doubleday, 1951), p. 63.

6. Lawrence, p. 72.

7. James Fenimore Cooper, *The Last of the Mohicans* (1826; rpt. New York: Scribner's, 1961), p. 359.

8. Lawrence, p. 73.

9. Jack Schaefer, *Shane* (Cambridge, Mass.: Riverside Press, 1949), p. 213.

10. Joe B. Frantz, "The Frontier Tradition: An Invitation to Violence," in *Violence in America: Historical and Comparative Perspectives; A Report to the National Commission on the Causes and Prevention of Violence, June 1969,* eds. Hugh Davis Graham and Ted Robert Gurr (New York: New American Library, 1969), p. 124.

11. Frantz, p. 122.

12. Raymond Chandler, "The Simple Art of Murder," in *The Simple Art of Murder* (1939; rpt. New York: Ballantine, 1972), p. 20.

13. "The Silver Age: Crime Fiction from Its Heyday Until Now," *The Times Literary Supplement,* February 25, 1955, p. xi.

14. G. K. Chesterton, "How to Write a Detective Story," in *The Spice of Life and Other Essays,* ed. Dorothy Collins (Beaconsfield, England: Darwin Finlayson, 1964), p. 19.

15. Dorothy Sayers, *The Omnibus of Crime* (New York: Harcourt, Brace, 1929), p. 9.

16. Edmund Wilson, "Who Cares Who Killed Roger Ackroyd?," in *A Literary Chronicle: 1920–1950* (Garden City, N.Y.: Doubleday, 1956), pp. 343–44.

17. Edmund Wilson, "Why Do People Read Detective Stories?," in *A Literary Chronicle: 1920–1950* (Garden City, N.Y.: Doubleday, 1956), p. 328.

18. W. H. Auden, "The Guilty Vicarage," in *The Dyer's Hand and Other Essays* (1956; rpt. New York: Knopf, 1968), p. 157.

19. Auden, p. 158,

20. G. K. Chesterton, "The Divine Detective," in *A Miscellany of Men* (New York: Dodd, Mead, 1912), p. 277.

21. David Abrahamsen, *Our Violent Society* (New York: Funk and Wagnalls, 1970), p. 187.

22. Robert Brown Parker, "The Violent Hero, Wilderness Heritage and Urban Reality: A Study of the Private Eye in the Novels of Dashiell Hammett, Raymond Chandler and Ross Macdonald." Diss., Boston University, 1971, p. 8.

23. Dashiell Hammett, *Red Harvest,* in *The Novels of Dashiell Hammett* (New York: Knopf, 1965), p. 142.

24. F. Scott Fitzgerald, *The Great Gatsby* (New York: Scribner's, 1925), p. 149.

25. John G. Cawelti, *The Six-Gun Mystique* (Bowling Green, Ohio: Bowling Green University Popular Press, 1973), p. 33.

26. Richard Maxwell Brown, "The American Vigilante Tradition," in *Violence in America: Historical and Comparative Perspectives; A Report to the National Commission on the Causes and Prevention of Violence, June 1969,* eds. Hugh Davis Green and Ted Robert Gurr (New York: New American Library, 1969), p. 193.

27. Richard Hofstadter, "Reflections on Violence in the United States," in *American Violence: A Documentary History* (New York: Knopf, 1971), p. 20.

28. Higgins, p. 345.

29. Leslie Fiedler, *Love and Death in the American Novel* (New York: Criterion, 1960), p. 476.

30. Raphael Patai, *Myth and the Modern Man* (Englewood Cliffs, N.J.: Prentice-Hall, 1972), p. 215.

31. Citations to Post are from "The Doomdorf Mystery," in *101 Years' Entertainment: The Great Detective Stories 1841–1941,* ed. Ellery Queen [Frederic Dannay and Manfred B. Lee] (New York: Little, Brown, 1941).

32. Quoted in Tage la Cour and Harald Mogensen, eds., *The Murder Book* (New York: Herder and Herder, 1971), p. 135.

33. Christopher LaFarge, "Mickey Spillane and His Bloody Hammer," *Saturday Review,* November 6, 1954, p. 56.

34. Archie H. Jones, "Cops, Robbers, Heroes and Anti-Heroes: The American Need to Create," *Journal of Popular Culture,* 1, No. 2 (Fall 1967), p. 122.

35. John G. Cawelti, "The Spillane Phenomenon," *Journal of Popular Culture,* 3, No. 1 (Summer 1969), p. 22.

36. Frantz, p. 130.

37. John Seelye, "Buckskin and Ballistics: William Leggett and the American Detective Story," *Journal of Popular Culture,* 1, No. 1 (Summer 1967), p. 53.

38. Fredric Wertham, *The Show of Violence* (1949; rpt. New York: Bantam, 1967), p. 190.

39. Russel Nye, *The Unembarrassed Muse: The Popular Arts in America* (New York: Dial Press, 1970), pp. 264–65.

40. Citations to Westlake's *Cops and Robbers* are from the New American Library reprint of the 1972 edition (New York, 1973).

41. Nicholas Blake [C. Day-Lewis], Introduction to *Murder for Pleasure: The Life and Times of the Detective Story*, Howard Haycraft (London: Peter Davies, 1942), p. xxi.

42. Raymond Chandler, *The Big Sleep* (1939; rpt. New York: Ballantine, 1971), p. 1.

43. Dorothy Gardiner and Katherine Sorley Walker, eds., *Raymond Chandler Speaking* (Freeport, N.Y.: Books for Libraries Press, 1962), p. 36.

TWO. The Sleepless Knight

"Short of murder, I'm clear."
—Archie Goodwin

History's first recorded private detective killed his first man at the age of fourteen. The occasion was a duel, the detective's name was Vidocq, and the dead man had been a fencing master.[1] The encounter was typical of the flamboyance that was to characterize the whole of Eugène-François Vidocq's life, a flamboyance probably at least in part attributable to the fact that our accounts of that life derive chiefly from the versions of Vidocq himself.

Born in 1775, by his fifteenth year he was a member of the Bourbon Regiment, and by the end of six months of that service he had credited himself with a duel for each of his years. Subsequently he distinguished himself by striking a sergeant-major and engaging in various desertions and reenlistments. He became an adept at cards and was eventually jailed for breach of the peace and forging a public document. He escaped from custody, was captured, escaped, was captured again, escaped again, served eight years in the galleys, and escaped again. He became an expert at disguise, on at least one occasion traveling convincingly as a nun. He tried schoolteaching briefly, but, as biographer John Philip Stead expressed it, "Some of the girl pupils were mature and provocative." [2] He was chased out of town. Shortly after he was shanghied in Holland and escaped again. He joined the crew of a French privateer and spent six months as a corsair; one day when the ship was in port he was arrested for being without the proper papers. By 1799 he found himself back at the courts of Bicêtre, from which he was relayed again to Douai prison—from which he escaped again. It was his twenty-fourth year.

After abortive attempts to become a merchant, Vidocq once more pursued the life of a corsair. At length, in an attempt to establish his respectability, he interviewed one M. Henry, head of the criminal department of the Paris *gendarmerie*, offering himself as a secret police spy. The offer, coupled as it was with a complete statement of his past history, was met with some suspicion. But Vidocq so impressed the authorities that he was hired

under Prefect of Police Dubois, and he became so successful that
by 1811 he had established a specialized security department of
police called the Sûreté, which became the basis for the modern
French organization still existent.

Vidocq's brigade of men, like himself, were not without evidence of interesting pasts. But it was Vidocq's phrase that one
should "set a thief to catch a thief," and records demonstrate his
crew of ex-cons served him well. Philip John Stead records the
tally:

> In 1817 Vidocq had twelve men working for him and be-
> tween them they made eight hundred and eleven arrests,
> including fifteen assassins, three hundred and forty-one
> thieves and thirty-eight receivers of stolen property. Fourteen
> escaped prisoners were recaptured, forty-three men who had
> broken their paroles were brought in and two hundred
> twenty-nine bad characters were arrested and banished from
> the city. Thirty-nine searches and seizures of stolen goods
> were made. Forty-six forgers, swindlers and confidence men
> were captured.[3]

Eventually Vidocq resigned his post in response to what appears
to have been jealous harassment from his more respected but less
successful colleagues. He employed convicts in his paper mill and
sat down to draft out his memoirs, from which source most of
the preceding obtains.

They were published in 1828 under the title *Mémoires de
Vidocq, chef de la police de sûreté jusqu'en 1827, aujord'hui pro-
prietaire et fabricant de papiers à Saint Mandé,* plugging his paper
factory. An English translation appeared the same year. But the
evidence suggests that the memoirs are not entirely his work—
Vidocq's education was spotty, pieced in as it was between physical
assaults and prison tours. He was not, however, by any means an
unimaginative man; at his mill he invented a forge-proof paper
and an indelible ink, and further employed his experiences to con-
struct an unburglarable door.[4] This same active imagination may
have embroidered the more mundane facts of his existence much
in the manner of the modern "Papillon," Henri Charrière. Certainly other hands worked up the four volumes of his autobiog-

raphy from notes supplied by Vidocq. The matter should not be one of concern to those seeking the influence rather than the reality of Vidocq's life. As Edwin Gile Rich observes in a preface to his translation,

> the importance of the book known as *The Memoirs of Vidocq* depends in no degree on who was the actual author. Ever since this material appeared in print, it has been a source of inspiration for some of the greatest works in literature. *Les Misérables* must be regarded as a direct descendant of Vidocq. The problem posed by Jean Valjean is clearly defined and emphasized again and again by Vidocq. In fact, whole chapters, scenes, pages of Hugo's masterpiece are stamped Vidocq. The *Vautrin* of Balzac [in *Le Père Goriot*], as the author freely acknowledged, is Vidocq. Dickens went to Vidocq for *Great Expectations*. Gaboriau's *Lecoq* [in *L'Affaire Lerouge, M. Lecoq,* etc.] was Vidocq himself. . . . Edgar Allan Poe and Conan Doyle were both fascinated by Vidocq, and the result in literature is a permanent contribution. Works of lesser note written in Vidocq's manner are innumerable. . . .[5]

Vidocq's eventful history did not end, however, with the writing of his memoirs. He was fifty-eight when he established the first recorded detective agency, *Le Bureau des Renseignements* (The Information Office), which was run in the manner of his *Sûreté* brigade—by thieves against thieves. Again the subsequent success of Vidocq's agency met with disfavor from the Prefecture, which resented the operation keenly. "To them," writes Stead, "it seemed that Vidocq had organized a counter-police, and in so far as he undertook work which the police would not or could not do, this was so." [6] Vidocq, the common man's advocate (his firm's motto was "Hatred of Rogues! Boundless devotion to trade!"), found himself once again persecuted by a professional aristocracy that envied him. Attempts were made to shut down the agency with charges of obtaining money on false pretenses, corrupting members of the civil service, and usurping police functions. Although he spent months in jail and substantial portions of his resources, Vidocq was ultimately exonerated.

The first significant American detective to begin an agency was

Allan Pinkerton, a man whose experience had been as severe as Vidocq's was uninhibited. Biographer James D. Horan notes that Pinkerton "had never tasted liquor, had never allowed it in his house, and had never smoked." [7] Originally a barrelmaker by profession, Pinkerton literally stumbled upon a counterfeiting ring while searching for lumber for his cooperage; he promptly led the local sheriff to their den and found he had stumbled upon a new profession as well. He was appointed Chicago's first official detective in 1849, became a special United States mail agent there shortly after, and opened his own agency in the same city in 1850. An early letterhead reveals the scope of the firm:

> Allan Pinkerton and Edward A. Rucker, under the style of Pinkerton & Co., have established an agency at Chicago, Illinois, for the purpose of transacting a General Detective Police Business in Illinois, Wisconsin, Michigan and Indiana; and will attend to the investigation and depredation [sic], frauds and criminal offenses; the detection of offenders, procuring arrests and convictions, apprehension or return of fugitives from justice, or bail; recovering lost or stolen property, obtaining information, etc. [8]

These functions were of course responsibilities incumbent upon the official police agencies of the states, but establishment police forces in 1850 were demonstrably inadequate. Horan observes further:

> At the time that Pinkerton formed his Agency, the nation's rural law enforcement consisted of entrepreneurs, bounty hunters, rural marshals, and sheriffs with casual deputies. Big-city police departments were mostly undermanned, politically dominated, and usually corrupt. [9]

At its best, the Pinkerton agency was effective; the firm seems to have performed valuable intelligence-gathering for the Union forces during the Civil War, and evidence suggests that Pinkerton himself may have been instrumental in aborting a plot by secessionists in Baltimore to assassinate President-elect Abraham Lincoln before his inauguration. [10] At its worst, the organization behaved in the wild tradition of vigilante justice; the notorious "bomb raid" on "Castle James," Jesse's home in Clay County, was attributed to Pinkerton leadership. The James boys were not at home, a circumstance that did not inhibit the raid: Jesse's mother and eight-year-old half-brother were. The mother lost an arm in the explosion, the boy his life. Guilty or not, Pinkerton was capable of declaring the results "merited and fearful punishment," [11] a noteworthy insight into the retributional bent of a relentless man. He was properly the original "private eye," adopting for his firm the emblem of an unwinking orb over the slogan "We Never Sleep."

As in the case of Vidocq, much of our information concerning the exploits of Pinkerton and his people is based on accounts by the detective. These accounts, while compelling as period pieces, rely too much on coincidence to be wholly reliable, although they are revelatory in regard to Pinkerton's vision of himself. But, like Vidocq's memoirs, the stories, true or not, were influential upon future fiction and are worthy of attention for that reason. Pinkerton's own preface to the series makes unacknowledged allowance for some stretching:

> "The Expressman and the Detective," and the other works announced by my publishers, are all *true stories*, transcribed from the records in my offices. If there be any incidental imbellishment, it is so slight that the actors in these scenes from the drama of life would never themselves detect it; and if the incidents seem to the reader at all marvelous or improbable, I can but remind him, in the words of the old adage, that "Truth is stranger than fiction." (p. i) [12]

If Pinkerton's version is stranger than either, *The Expressman and the Detective* (1875) remains one of the earliest nonfictional American accounts of the private eye in action, and not surprisingly it introduces two essential qualities of the private eye novel to come. The first of these is an insistence upon a hero. Pinkerton may follow the adventures of other agents, but never without establishing his own primal presence. Explaining the background of a case in hand, he modestly reverts from first to third person:

> [The client] said he knew of only one man who could bring
> out the robbery, and he was living in Chicago.
>   Pinkerton was the name of the man he referred to. (p. 16)

In case the reader was wondering. And when the request is made
for him to send on assignment someone "one-half horse and one-
half alligator," the sleuth has pause for serious reflection:

> It was hard to decide what kind of a man to send! I wanted to
> send the very best, and would gladly go myself, but did not
> know whether the robbery was important enough to demand
> my personal attention. (p. 18)

It was not.

The second quality of *The Expressman* essential to the future
private cop story is the immersion of the eye into an almost sur-
real under-world, an underworld to which he must adapt in order
to get his work done. The danger of assuming an unsavory role is
immediate: between the authentic hood and the ersatz, how long
can a distinction be maintained?

> Maroney [the suspect] frequented a saloon kept by a man I
> will call Patterson. Patterson's saloon was the fashionable
> drinking resort of Montgomery, and was frequented by all
> the fast men in town. Although outwardly a very quiet, respect-
> able place, inwardly, as Porter [the operative] found, it was
> far from reputable. Up stairs were private rooms, in which
> gentlemen met to have a quiet game of poker; while down
> stairs could be found the greenhorn, just "roped in," and
> being swindled, at *three card monte*. There were, also, rooms
> where the "young bloods" of the town—as well as the old—
> could meet ladies of easy virtue. It was frequented by fast men
> from New Orleans, Mobile, and other places, who were con-
> tinually arriving and departing.
>   I advised the General Superintendent that it would be best
> to have Porter get in touch with the "bloods" of the town,
> make himself acquainted with any ladies Maroney or his wife
> might be familiar with, and adopt generally the character of
> a fast man. (p. 25)

The operative then is an extralegal agent sent out as arbiter into a world that has lost control of itself. He is alone because he can rely on no one, especially the authorities, and the law he subscribes to is one outside that world but given sharp definition only by his conduct—which must emulate the worst elements of that world.

These considerations are reinforced in a subsequent work of Pinkerton's, *The Molly Maguires and the Detectives* (1877), which was to influence Conan Doyle's last Sherlock Holmes novel (*The Valley of Fear*, 1915). In October 1873 Pinkerton was approached in Philadelphia by F. B. Gowen, the president of the Philadelphia and Reading Railway Company. His story was one of municipal incapacity and murder amok:

> "The coal regions are infested by a most desperate class of men, banded together for the worst purposes—called, by some, the Buchanans, by others the Molly Maguires—and they are making sad havoc with the country. It is a secret organization, has its meetings in hidden and out-of-the-way places, and its members . . . are guilty of a majority of the murders and other deeds of outrage which, for many years, have been committed in the neighborhood. I wish you to investigate this mysterious order, find out its interior workings, [and] expose its evil transactions. . . . Municipal counties are powerless, and the usual run of detectives are of as little value as the open, uniformed police of the different cities. All these have been tested, and all have failed." (pp. 13–14) [13]

Gowen's emphasis is on the inadequacy of conventional legal procedures, demanding more direct methods. The private detective then becomes a vigilante's messenger, if not by choice, then by necessity. For the sanctioned sources of justice are not only inoperative, they are corrupt:

> "The Mollies rule our people with a rod of iron. They do this and make no sign. The voice of the fraternity is unheard, but the work is performed. Even the political sentiments of the commonwealth are moulded by them, and in their particular field they elect or defeat whomsoever they may please.

They control, in a measure, the finances of the state. Their
chiefs direct affairs this way, and that way, without hinder-
ance. Men without an iota of moral principle, they dictate
the principles of otherwise honorable parties. In its ultimate
results this complexion of affairs in Pennsylvania touches,
to a considerable degree, the interests of the whole country.
Wherever anthracite is employed is also felt the vise-like grip
of this midnight, dark-lantern, murderous-minded fraternity."
(p. 15)

The impact of all of this of course serves to magnify Pinkerton's
assignment in his own mind and in the minds of his readers, but
it also creates an atmosphere of evil commensurate with a sense
of the *holiness* of the mission and its necessity for the sanctity of
moral order. Under such conditions, anything goes. Pinkerton's
reflections on the request of a citizen's committee are closer to
those of an avenging angel than to those of an objective professional:

I had heard of many assassinations by these Molly Maguires,
and also about those performed by the Ku-Klux and similar
combinations in the Southern States. It had always seemed
to me that it was a sacred duty which Pennsylvania owed to
herself, to her citizens, and to the country at large, to clear
her garments of the taint resting upon them and bring to
punishment the persons who, for so many years, habitually
outraged decency, spilt human blood without stint, and con-
verted the richest section of one of the most wealthy and
refined of all the sisterhood of States into a very golgotha—
a locality from which law-abiding men and women might soon
be forced to flee, as from the threatened cities of the plain, or
from a spot stricken with plague and pestilence.
"I will enter upon the business . . . !" (p. 16)

In *Molly Maguires* one again has the sense of witnessing a
personal voyage into the moral maelstrom. As agent McParland
begins his assignment, changing identities to meld into the symbol-
ically jet world of the coal man, there occurs a passage relating his

journey down into the mines that takes on the archetypal proportions of a Daliesque descent into hell:

> For a brief period they were in total darkness, and a sensation, as of seasickness, came over him. Still he clung to his support and the uncomfortable feeling soon left him. As the lower regions were reached, the traveler thought he would be far more content if again breathing the clear ether above. The system experienced absolute relief when the motion ceased, and the solid bottom of the shaft was touched. But here it was like entering a new sphere. There was dark above, below, and all around, only here and there relieved by dim little stars, which were continually dodging downward, sidewise, and upward, as though held by an unsteady hand. As his eyes acquired familiarity with the situation, he saw that to each one of these erratic satellites was attached the body of a living man—in fact, they were only diminutive lamps which the miners and their helpers wore above their hats to light them in their labors. (p. 53)

In *Molly Maguires* one also has an awareness of the detective as extraordinary man, as hero—a hero of sometimes ambiguous qualities. For though his prowess is larger than life, his chameleon ethical sense must raise questions about the kind of heroism he objectifies. Meditating on the abilities necessary to fulfill the assignment, Pinkerton draws this picture of an ideal agent:

> My detective should become, to all intents and purposes, one of the order, and continue so while he remains in the case before us. He should be hardy, tough, and capable of laboring, in season and out of season, to accomplish, unknown to those about him, a single absorbing object. (p. 17)

Thus he is a man whose solitary consuming loyalty must be to the job, the soldier's unquestioning responsibility for successful accomplishment of his mission. To do this the detective must be a prudent man, one "able to distinguish the real from the ideal moral obligation, and pierce the vail [sic] separating a supposed from an actual state of affairs" (p. 19). The distinction between "real" moral obligations and "ideal" ones seems to be the distinction between expeditious behavior and the more finicky ethical kind. The agent presumably will not allow fine philosophical constructs to get between him and his work. Indeed, nothing less than apostasy is required of him. As Pinkerton makes clear, such an agent must be as one

> who could make almost a new man of himself, take his life in his hands, and enter upon a work which was apparently against those bound to him by close ties of nationality, if not of blood and kindred; and for months, perhaps for years, place himself in antagonism with and rebellion against the dictates of his church—the church which from his earliest breath he has been taught to revere. He would perforce obtain a reputation for evil conduct, from which it was doubtful that he could ever entirely extricate himself. . . . He must face the priest, and endure the bad opinion of his countrymen even until the end. For an indefinite period he was to be one dead and buried in the grave—dead to his family and friends—sinking his individuality—and be published abroad as the companion and associate of assassins, murderers, incendiaries, thieves and gamblers. In no other way could I hope to secure admission to the inner circle of this labyrinth of iniquity. (p. 21)

Lastly, the detective must be answerable to no man or organization for his movements. As a free agent, Pinkerton demands of his employers that "he shall not become known to any person as a detective." He adds a further proviso: "Take the precaution that my name, and those of my superintendents and employes, do not appear upon any of your books." And yet another: "Further, whatever may be the result of the examination, no person in my employ . . . shall ever be required to appear and give testimony upon the witness stand" (p. 18). The Pinkerton man's accountability is removed simultaneously with his personal identity.

If the detective therefore is a social and individual law unto himself, the argument implies, it is in the interests of justice that he be so—restrictions impair efficiency. Perhaps the only authority remaining is that of Pinkerton himself as employer, the angry god whose high Olympus is the home office: "I was, if possible, to destroy the Molly Maguires. Therefore, my operatives must be the instruments of that destruction" (p. 21).

They were. But even the most laudatory accounts of their work, especially concerning the performance of agent McParland, contain uncomfortable phrases. Richard Wilmer Rowan's purple history of the Pinkerton success closes with this passage:

> [McParland's] exploit in detective annals has marched steadily on to fame. Because he was plausible and resolute, audacious—unscrupulous, if you will—the Molly Maguires and the dread of a decade in Pennsylvania were swept away to the limbo of evils that have been.[14]

If such encomiums are descriptive of angels, surely they are fallen ones.

The narratives of Vidocq and Pinkerton established quasi-nonfictionally what was to become a fictional type: the private eye. The Vidocq-Pinkerton figure owes his existence to the inadequacy of the organized police; he outperforms them and is admired and consequently resented by them. He is unencumbered by the civil law because it is his conviction that he represents a higher one, largely self-defined—his justice is surer. He is smarter than his adversaries, he is aware of the underworld, and he can submerge himself at will into the criminal sink. His street knowledge is profound. Although he may serve an agency, he works alone and answers to no one—certainly not to the client, and only perhaps to his boss. These qualities were refined and extended by later writers.

Two varieties of detective created themselves out of the Vidocq-Pinkerton memoirs. The flamboyance of Vidocq contributed the detective as aesthete, a "criminologist" of bizarre habits who pursued criminals out of a fascination for the reasoning process. Usually a talented amateur, his function was to solve the unending problems of a blundering police, often without remuneration or even credit. The more successful practitioners of the aesthetic school were English, although an American began it and other Americans contributed. Edgar Allan Poe's Dupin fit this pattern,

as did Conan Doyle's Sherlock Holmes and S. S. Van Dine's Philo
Vance. Allan Pinkerton's more matter-of-fact approach was responsible for the second variety, the detective as working man. This
more professional figure either worked for an agency or was self-
employed, and his investigative motive was clearly money rather
than the exercise of his mind. The police did not consult him; he
was viewed as an intrusion rather than as an assistance. A relatively
poor man, he found little romance and a lot of ugliness in his
labors, but he continued to perform them because he found an
affinity for the work. The best examples of this category are all
American and include Dashiell Hammett's Sam Spade, Raymond
Chandler's Philip Marlowe, and Ross Macdonald's Lew Archer.

Edgar Allan Poe is generally credited with having written the
first detective story. "The Murders in the Rue Morgue" appeared
in *Graham's Magazine* in April 1841. The story concerns an
"analyst" named C. Auguste Dupin who appeared in two subsequent Poe tales, "The Mystery of Marie Rogêt" (1842) and "The
Purloined Letter" (1844).[15] Dupin's performance in these three
stories established the basis for the detective-as-aesthete school that
dominated mystery fiction until the 1920s. Although Dupin refers
to Vidocq patronizingly as "a good guesser" and "a persevering
man" (p. 166),[16] Poe's debt to his predecessor is clear both in the
nature of his hero's work and in the Parisian locale.

"The Murders in the Rue Morgue" begins as a treatise on
"analytical power," asserting that real perception depends upon
imaginative observation. "The necessary knowledge is that of
what to observe" (p. 148). What follows is intended, Poe writes,
to be "a commentary upon the proposition just advanced" (p. 150).
The result is an illustration of the imaginative man, Dupin, suc-
ceeding in the solution of a problem that defeats one merely
scientific, Prefect of Police G____.

The anonymous narrator of "Murders" begins with his introduction to Dupin, a man whose familial disfavor, deprived circumstances, and literary enthusiasms are reminiscent of Poe's own:

This young gentleman was of an excellent—indeed of an
illustrious—family, but, by a variety of untoward events, had
been reduced to such poverty that the energy of his character
succumbed beneath it, and he ceased to bestir himself in the

world, or to care for the retrieval of his fortunes. By courtesy of his creditors, there still remained in his possession a small remnant of his patrimony; and, upon the income arising from this, he managed, by means of a rigorous economy, to procure the necessaries of life, without troubling himself about its superfluities. Books, indeed, were his sole luxuries. . . . p. (150)

At contact with Dupin, the narrator is consumed with admiration: "I felt my soul enkindled within me by the wild fervor, and the vivid freshness of his imagination." The two discover a kindred sympathy and rent "a time-eaten and grotesque mansion, long deserted," and the narrator admits to a certain unconventionality in their life style:

> Had the routine of our life at this place been known to the world, we should have been regarded as madmen. . . . Our seclusion was perfect. We admitted no visitors. Indeed the locality of our retirement had been carefully kept a secret from my own former associates. . . . We existed within ourselves alone. (p. 151)

In these even more cynical days, one is led inexorably to conclusions of some dubious sexual relationship between Dupin and his friend, but their association has aspects even more *outré* than that. Both men share Poe's fascination for gloom; indeed, virtually the whole of the story is told in the dark:

> It was a freak of fancy in my friend . . . to be enamored of the Night for her own sake; and into this *bizarrerie,* as into all his others, I quickly fell. . . . At the first dawn of the morning we closed all the mossy shutters of our old building; lighted a couple of tapers which, strongly perfumed, threw out only the ghastliest and feeblest of rays. By the aid of these we then busied our souls in dreams—reading, writing, or conversing, until warned by the clock of the advent of true Darkness. Then we sallied forth into the streets, arm and arm. . . . (pp. 151–52)

Dupin as dreamer of dark dreams becomes our intermediary in a nightmare, insisting upon the logic of an apparently insane world. The detective's response to horror is that "an inquiry will afford us amusement" (p. 167); thus the locked room murder of an old woman and her daughter, marked by maniacal brutality and strange voices overheard in a chamber at the top of the stairs, becomes the unfortunate result of a lost monkey's chance encounter with an open shutter.

If Dupin carries on a vision of the private detective as independent arbiter of evil, Dupin's view of Prefect of Police G____ and his minions condemns again the authorities as inadequate even when they are not foolish.

> "The Parisian police, so much extolled for *acumen*, are cunning, but no more. There is no method in their proceedings, beyond the method of the moment. They make a vast parade of measures; but, not infrequently, these are . . . ill adapted to the objects proposed. . . ." (p. 165)

In this story, as in much of detective fiction to come, "the police are entirely at fault" (p. 165). In the final paragraph, Dupin allows himself a last Parthian twit at the hapless G____:

> "Our friend the Prefect is somewhat too cunning to be profound. In his wisdom is no *stamen*. It is all head and no body, like the pictures of the Goddess Laverna,—or, at best, all head and shoulders, like a codfish. But he is a good creature after all." (p. 192)

These motifs are continued in the two other Dupin stories. In "The Mystery of Marie Rogêt," Dupin expounds what Poe purported to be the solution of an actual murder of a young girl in New York, although recent scholarship suggests Poe's answer was adjusted to fit evidence that emerged subsequent to his writing.[17] This time Dupin is sought out by Prefect G____ and evidently hired to do the prefect's work for him:

> [G____] had been piqued by the failure of all his endeavors to ferret out the assassins. His reputation—so he said with a

peculiarly Parisian air—was at stake. Even his honor was concerned. The eyes of the public were upon him; and there was really no sacrifice which he would not be willing to make for the development of the mystery. He concluded a somewhat droll speech with a compliment upon what he was pleased to term the *tact* of Dupin, and made him a direct, and certainly a liberal proposition, the precise nature of which I do not feel myself at liberty to disclose. . . .[18]

Dupin discourses at length upon natural law and drowned bodies and finally determines the murderer to have been a naval officer. The next Dupin story, "The Purloined Letter," again begins with the distressed G_____ asking for amateur counsel. A compromising letter has been stolen by a diplomat and hidden somewhere in his apartments. The prefect confesses himself unable to find it and enlists Dupin's aid. The tale once more becomes the account of a contest between the imaginative man and the empirical—poet versus scientist. G_____ at one point describes a poet as "one remove from a fool," to which Dupin responds modestly that he has "been guilty of a little doggerel" himself (p. 34).[19] While G_____'s method has been the thorough search of the diplomat's house, according to the best investigative training, Dupin's approach is to reflect that a man of his adversary's intellect would very likely hide a letter in a letter rack, too obvious a location for serious scrutiny. There is the element of whimsy in this attack, befitting a man who disputes "the reason educed by mathematical study" (p. 44). When Dupin places the letter in G_____'s hands (after duly accepting fifty thousand francs in payment), G_____ behaves as he might be expected to:

> [he] grasped it in a perfect agony of joy, opened it with a trembling hand, cast a rapid glance at its contents, and then, scrambling and struggling to the door, rushed at length unceremoniously from the room. . . . (p. 39)

Sherlock Holmes, the world's first and "only official consulting detective," considered Dupin "a very inferior fellow" (p. 14) [20] but was not averse to using his methods. The creation of Sir Arthur Conan Doyle, Holmes first appeared in *A Study in Scarlet,* printed in the twenty-eighth issue of *Beeton's Christmas Annual* for 1887.[21] The three Holmes novels and sixty short stories that followed established Doyle's creation as a folk hero and shaped the direction of detective fiction for years to come. Immediate imitations like Arthur Morrison's Martin Hewitt (*The Chronicles of Martin Hewitt*, 1895) proliferated during Doyle's lifetime; later, pastiches like the Solar Pons stories of August Derleth (*The Case Book of Solar Pons*, 1965) continued to be written and read all over the world. Holmes, like Dupin, is an inveterate eccentric; like Dupin, he suffers the attentions of a biographer; and, most like Dupin, he has a supreme distrust for the imaginative capability of the civil force.

A Study in Scarlet recounts Dr. John H. Watson's initial encounter with his subject. If Dupin is a variety of Byron's romantic, pale and isolate in a rotting room, Holmes is the marriage of *fin de siècle* aestheticism and the Victorian deification of science, the former accounting for his habits, the latter for his procedures.

> In height he was rather over six feet, and so excessively lean that he seemed to be considerably taller. His eyes were sharp and piercing, save during these intervals of torpor to which I have alluded; and his thin, hawk-like nose gave his whole expression an air of alertness and decision. His chin, too, had the prominence and squareness which mark the man of determination. His hands were invariably blotted with ink and stained with chemicals, yet he was possessed of extraordinary delicacy of touch, as I frequently had occasion to observe when I watched him manipulate his fragile philosophical instruments. (p. 9)

Holmes's addiction to cocaine and the violin, his fondness for indoor revolver practice, and impatience with routine mark him a bohemian, but his faith in empiricism and methodological process places him in more systematic company. Watson records his fascination with the deductive process as a sense of the infinite interpretability of life:

> "From a drop of water . . . a logician could infer the possibility of an Atlantic or a Niagara without having seen or

heard of one or the other. So all life is a great chain, the nature of which is known whenever we are shown a single link of it. Like all other arts, the Science of Deduction and Analysis is one which can only be acquired by long and patient study. . . . [I]t sharpens the faculties of observation, and teaches one where to look and what to look for. By a man's finger-nails, by his coatsleeve, by his boots, by his trouser-knees, by the callosities of his four fingers and thumb, by his expression, by his shirt-cuffs—by each of these things a man's calling is plainly revealed. That all united should fail to enlighten the competent inquirer in any case is almost inconceivable." (p. 13)

This is of course the art of the diagnostician; Doyle, like his interface Watson, was a medical man, and Holmes seems to have been drawn from a former Edinburgh University instructor of the author's, Dr. Joseph Bell.

The personal aberrations of Holmes—his drug-taking, lotuspose meditation, arcane monograph writing, and the like—serve to make human what otherwise approaches the inhuman. Holmes is not a demonstrative man.

All emotions, and that one [sexual love] particularly, were abhorrent to his cold, precise but admirably balanced mind. He was, I take it, the most perfect reasoning and observing machine that the world has seen, but as a lover he would have placed himself in a false position. He never spoke of the softer passions, save with a gibe and a sneer. They were admirable things for the observer—excellent for drawing the veil from men's motives and actions. But for the trained reasoner to admit such intrusions into his own delicate and finely adjusted temperament was to introduce a distracting factor which might throw a doubt upon all his mental results. (p. 177)

The cold, precise quality of mind was an essential element in the detective-as-aesthete school, the tenor of which inclined more toward fantasy than realism. Jacques Futrelle carried it to exponential lengths in his ingenious series of tales concerning Professor Augustus S. F. X. Van Dusen, "The Thinking Machine," who wore a number eight hat and a perennially forbidding squint (*The Thinking Machine On the Case,* 1908). This supracerebral tendency was intended to convey credibly the kind of surpassing Sherlockian individual capable of employing "immense faculties and extraordinary powers of observation in following out those clues, and clearing up those mysteries which had been abandoned as hopeless by the official police" (p. 177).

Holmes's attitude toward his professional competition is at least as mordant as Dupin's. Early in *A Study in Scarlet* he expresses this opinion of the inspector requesting his services:

> "Gregson is the smartest of the Scotland Yarders . . . ; he and Lestrade are the pick of a bad lot. They are both quick and energetic, but conventional—shockingly so. . . . Supposing I unravel the whole matter, you may be sure that Gregson, Lestrade and Co. will pocket all the credit." (p. 17)

In another story, his sentiments are these:

> "Inspector Gregory, to whom the case has been committed, is an extremely competent officer. Were he but gifted with imagination he might rise to great heights in his profession." (p. 387)

And in one more, these:

> "That you, Lestrade?" said Holmes.
> "Yes, Mr. Holmes. I took the job myself. It's good to see you back in London, sir."
> "I think you want a little unofficial help. Three undetected murders in one year won't do, Lestrade. But you handled the Molesey Mystery with less than your usual—that's to say, you handled it fairly well." (p. 571)

The Holmes novels did not meet with immediate success. *A Study in Scarlet* and its sequel, *The Sign of Four* (1890), caused little critical stir, but the regular appearance of short stories about Holmes in the *Strand Magazine,* beginning with "A Scandal in Bohemia" in July 1891, received enthusiastic attention. As an interesting retelling of "The Purloined Letter," "A Scandal" reveals the extent of Doyle's debt to Poe. These stories became so popular that the author had his hero killed off in 1893, sending him over the falls of Reichenbach locked in the arms of "the Napolean of crime" to enable Doyle to return to writing historical fiction. Protest against "The Final Problem" was so overwhelming that Doyle wrote *The Hound of the Baskervilles* (1902) to mollify his public; and later he resurrected his hero in "The Adventure of the Empty House" (1903). The stories appeared again regularly until the publication of the last one, "The Adventure of Shoscombe Old Place," in March 1927.[23]

Although Holmes was made to say on one occasion that "it's every man's business to see justice done" (p. 484), unlike his future American heirs he appeared to be more interested in mercy than in justice. His extralegal activities usually extended to preventing prosecution rather than personally carrying it out. The detective suppresses evidence in "The Boscombe Valley Mystery" (1891) that would convict an aging murderer in order to protect the reputation of a dying man. In "The Adventure of Charles Augustus Milverton" (1904), Holmes witnesses the killing of an extortionist and refuses to pursue the woman who did it. In each instance the victim was a blackmailer; blackmail had to be the unforgivable Victorian crime in a society surviving on the appearance of rectitude. Although he saw the law and its defenders as flawed, the English private eye was more protector than enforcer.

Not so the American version. S. S. Van Dine's dilettantish Philo Vance was an unlikely minister of vengeance, but even in the drawing-room novels that made him the best-selling favorite of Franklin Roosevelt rough justice prevailed. Van Dine (the pseudonym of Willard Huntington Wright) wrote that "all good detective novels have had for their protagonist a character of attractiveness and interest, of high and fascinating attainments—a man at once human and unusual, colorful and gifted." [24] Philo Vance was Van Dine's idea of such a character. He bore a disturbing resemblance to Holmes:

He was just under six feet, slender, sinewy, and graceful.
His chiselled regular features gave his face the attraction of

strength and uniform modelling, but a sardonic coldness of expression precluded the designation of handsome. He had aloof gray eyes, a straight, slender nose, and a mouth suggesting both cruelty and asceticism.[25]

He was bloodless like Holmes—and, like Holmes, a man with a passion for arcane minutiae:

He was something of an authority on Japanese and Chinese prints; he knew tapestries and ceramics; and once I heard him give an impromptu *causerie* to a few guests on Tanagora figurines which, had it been transcribed, would have made a most delightful and interesting monograph.[26]

Also like Holmes, Vance's exploits are recounted by a biographer, "Van Dine" himself, who, as the detective's legal and financial adviser, follows him slavishly about. More effacing even than Watson, "Van Dine" never in the course of a dozen novels utters a single word. Rather, he restricts himself to a meticulous recounting of Vance's movements and comments. These comments are delivered in an accent which is labeled Oxonian, but which, upon examination, resembles no recognizable tongue in the civilized world. An example:

"By the by," he said, slipping into his coat, "I note that our upliftin' press bedecked its front pages this morning with head-lines about a pogrom at the old Greene mansion last night. Wherefore?" [27]

Another: ". . . I'm happy to note that crime is picking up again. It's a deuced drab world without a nice murky murder now and then, don't y' know." [28] A smoker of rose petal-tipped *Régie* cigarettes, eater of *truffes gastronome* with Madeira sauce, devotee of the Hispano-Suiza and translator of Delacroix, the monocled Vance is a caricature of Poe's Dupin given the mobility and function of Doyle's Holmes. He shares their mutual passion for cold reason: "Until we can approach all human problems . . . with the clinical aloofness and cynical contempt of a doctor examining a guinea-pig strapped to a board, we have little chance of getting at the truth." [29] And he shares as well their supreme confidence in the application of analysis to crime: "Just as an expert aesthetician can analyze a picture and tell you who painted it, so can the expert psychologist analyze a crime and tell you who committed it. . . ." [30]

Vance first appears in *The Benson Murder Case* (1926) and is immediately placed in a position superior to the police. As a friend of District Attorney Markham, Vance is called in whenever a crime is committed that defeats the ratiocinative powers of the authorities—that is to say, he is called in all the time. Vance's opinion of his official rivals is predictably scornful: "I say, Markham, . . . it has always been a source of amazement to me how easily you investigators of crime are misled by what you call clues. You find a footprint, or a parked automobile, or a monogrammed handkerchief, and then dash off on a wild chase with your eternal *Ecce signum!*" [31] Pontificates Philo: "The only crimes that are ever solved are those planned by stupid people." [32] The Law is usually represented by the stolid Sergeant Heath, who pursues the obvious with the unrelenting assiduousness of a process server in a one-reeler. Heath in moments of indecision is prone to divest himself of outbursts like these: "What's on the cards? Where do we go from here? I need action." [33] Vance is moved at such junctures to grieve: "And it's stubborn, unimaginative chaps like Heath who constitute the human barrage between the criminal and society! . . . Sad, sad." [34]

It is perhaps even sadder that the only intervening supportive bulwark is Vance, for he takes some little time to catch his man —often at the cost of numerous lives in the interim. At the outset of *The Greene Murder Case* (1927), Vance is summoned to investigate a murder and shooting at the home of a decadent upperclass family. By the time he uncovers the killer a further assault has occurred and three more murders, reducing his viable list of suspects to three. These executions proceed as Vance commits himself to musings such as the following: ". . . Some deep, awful motive lies behind that crime. There are depths beneath depths in what happened last night—obscure fetid chambers of the human soul. Black hatreds, unnatural desires, hideous impulses, obscene ambitions are at the bottom of it. . . ." [35] When he does at long last corner the killer he withholds his knowledge that she is in possession of cyanide capsules; this permits her to kill herself in the very presence of the district attorney. The two surviving suspects then embrace and sail for the Riviera.

Vance's tendency to help justice along is at its apogee in *The Bishop Murder Case* (1929). Here he does not assist a suicide—he engineers one. Before breaking into one suspect's home, Vance engages in this discussion of legal procedure:

> Markham rushed forward and caught him round the shoulders.
> "Are you mad?" he exclaimed. "You're breaking the law."
> "The law!" There was scathing irony in Vance's retort. "We're dealing with a monster who sneers at all law. You may coddle him if you care to, but I'm going to search that attic if it means spending the rest of my life in jail. —Sergeant, open that door!" [36]

His haste may in part spring from the usual concatenation of killings in the course of a lingering Vance investigation, but some of it is vendetta as well. When Vance arranges for the murderer to quaff a dram of poison—again in the presence of the D.A.—Markham exhibits growing impatience.

> "You took the law into your own hands!"
> "I took it in my arms—it was helpless. . . . But don't be so righteous. Do you bring a rattlesnake to the bar of justice? Do you give a mad dog his day in court? I felt no more compunction in aiding a monster like Dillard into the Beyond than I would have in crushing out a poisonous reptile in the act of striking."
> "But it was murder!" exclaimed Markham in horrified indignation.
> "Oh, doubtless," said Vance cheerfully.[37]

What Markham has overlooked is the initial stricture Vance demanded on his first appearance. If the authorities wanted his help, Vance warned, "I must have your word you'll give me every possible assistance, and will refrain from all profound legal objections." [38] The principal difference between Vance and his quarry seems to reside only in the number of victims; under the dandy's mask is a killer as cold-blooded as the major who murders bald Alvin Benson or the heiress who thins out the Greene family or the "bishop" who bumps off his rivals with a bow and arrow.

Firmly seated between the aesthetic and working schools is Rex Stout's unclassifiable Nero Wolfe, who performed his debut in *Fer-de-Lance* (1934) and survives still in more than sixty sequels. (Stout's paperback sales alone count for thirteen million Wolfe volumes to date.) Wolfe works, but only to support his extravagant tastes. Legman and amanuensis Archie Goodwin carries on the recording role of a Watson without Watson's humorless, flannel-brained stolidity. Still, Wolfe's grand manner and catalog of personal grotesqueries keep him nearer the ruff than the white collar.

Wolfe bears a close resemblance to Sherlock Holmes's older brother Mycroft, who was introduced at the Diogenes Club in "The Greek Interpreter" (1893) as the great detective's "superior in observation and deduction" (p. 503). Mycroft was "absolutely corpulent" (p. 504) and possessed of "no energy" (p. 503); Wolfe weighs in at a seventh of a ton and seldom strays from his New York brownstone home. Like Mycroft, Wolfe has others do his clue chasing, reserving as his function armchair analysis only. These similarities and others have led critics like William S. Baring-Gould to suggest that more than a literary connection links the two; Baring-Gould chooses to regard Nero Wolfe as the generous issue of Sherlock Holmes and *femme fatale* Irene Adler ("A Scandal in Bohemia"),[39] and the hypothesis has received no direct challenge from Stout.

Wolfe's peculiarities, however, far exceed Mycroft's. His gargantuan capacity can accommodate six quarts of beer a day and half a sheep in two, cooked twenty different ways. His girth accounts for the elevator he has installed to transport him up and down the three floors of his house, the top of which contains his capacious plant rooms ("one for Cattleyas, Laelias and hybrids, one for Odontoglossums, Oncidiums and Miltonia hybrids, and the tropical room")[40] where he attends orchids four hours daily. Wolfe affects canary-yellow shirts and purses his lips out when he thinks. "He likes no woman." [41] A hater of slang, he is a master of verbal punctilio and even something of an epigrammatist: "A pessimist gets nothing but pleasant surprises, an optimist nothing but unpleasant." [42]

Archie Goodwin, Wolfe's assistant, is more conventional. Slender and unaddicted to literature, Goodwin expresses preferences for milk and eight hours of sleep. "I'm handsome," he admits, "but I'm not just handsome." [43] His tendencies lean toward combat and perfunctory lechery. Goodwin is the capable animated half of the team. As he expresses it: "Genius is fine for the ignition spark, but to get there someone has to see that the radiator doesn't leak and no tire is flat." [44] Goodwin is the hard-boiled hero with corporate allegiances.

Fer-de-Lance offers interesting contradictions in Wolfe's character. "I would not pose as a ruffian," he avows, "and I suffer from a romantic conscience" (p. 207).[45] Yet he is able to assert as easily, "I am not a public servant, I am not a member of the bar, and I have sworn to uphold no law. The dangerous position of an accessory after the fact does not impress me" (p. 103). His empathy for suffering is extreme:

He hated flies and very few ever got in there, but two had somehow made it and were fooling around on his desk. Much as he hated them, he couldn't kill them; he said that while a live fly irritated him to the point of hatred, a killed one outraged his respect for the dignity of death, which was worse. (p. 146)

Yet that empathy is somehow selective:

"As long as I live [admits Goodwin] I'll never forget the time he had a bank president pinched, or rather I did, on no evidence whatever except that the fountain pen on his desk was dry. I was never so relieved in my life as when the guy shot himself an hour later." (p. 64)

Despite his squeamishness about the death of flies, Wolfe will by the end of the novel choreograph the deaths of two men. Once again Wolfe's story is the story of a man who invents moral cause for his own illegality while the authorities look on in resentful awe ("You're a lulu, Mr. Wolfe" [p. 36]). These authorities are represented without distinction as usual by O'Grady of Homicide ("Cerebrally an oaf" [p. 40]) and Anderson of the D.A.'s office ("He would admit that he owes you something only if the doors were closed and he whispered in your ear. Married money" [p. 41]).

Fer-de-Lance concerns the murder of a university president named Barstow who is shot at a golf match with a poisoned needle from a number one wood. His wife is quick to seek amends; she offers fifty thousand dollars for information leading to the discovery and "righteous punishment" of the killer. Wolfe complies. As he observes at one point, "Remember that those of us who are both civilized and prudent commit our murders only under the complicated rules which permit us to avoid personal responsibility" (p. 264). When it becomes clear that Barstow borrowed the rigged club just prior to his turn on the tee, Wolfe concludes the owner, grain broker E. D. Kimball, was the intended victim and Kimball's pilot son, Manuel, the murderer. Here Manuel promptly takes his father up in an open-cockpit twin-motor and deliberately flies the both of them into the ground. Wolfe promptly admits he was behind it all:

> "I helped to remedy that error [of Barstow's death]. I had Durkin deliver to Manuel Kimball copies of our evidence against him, and I telephoned Manuel Kimball that he was surrounded, on the earth and above the earth. I left it to nature to proceed, having ascertained that E. D. Kimball was at home and would not leave that morning." (p. 311)

"You killed him," Archie concludes brightly. But Wolfe maintains his actions constituted kindness, not cruelty:

> "Manuel had tried to kill his father. By an accident beyond his control the innocent Barstow had been killed instead. Evidence that would convict Manuel of murder was in my possession. How should I use it? . . . If I had permitted you to get Manuel Kimball, without warning, and deliver him alive to the vengeance of the people of the State of New York, he would have gone to the chair of judicial murder a bitter and defeated man, his heart empty of the one deep satisfaction

life had offered to it; and his father, equally bitter and no less
defeated, would have tottered through some few last years
with nothing left to trade." (pp. 311–12)

Wolfe's procedure is certainly tidier and more immediate than
that of the courts, but one is led to wonder if the "vengeance of
the people of the State of New York" could have been any more
terrible than that of the incomparable Nero. "The only way I
knew it had been E. D. Kimball," notes Archie at the crash site,
"was that it was mixed up with a strap in the position of the back
seat . . ." (p. 307).

Wolfe strikes again in a later novelette entitled "Booby Trap"
(1942). After being called in by G-2 as a "civilian consultant" to
uncover a betrayer of "industrial processes" to the enemy, the
ham-handed hawkshaw finds himself embroiled in the grenade
murder of an army colonel. Inspector Cramer is of course at hand,
but as Wolfe observes, "Mr. Cramer is constantly leaping at the
throat of evil and finding himself holding on for dear life to the
tip of its tail" (p. 140).[46] Exit Cramer. Wolfe determines the culprit to be none other than Congressman John Bell Shattuck, af-
filiation tactfully unspecified. Wolfe and Goodwin drive Shattuck
to a park in the company of another grenade. The fat man explains reasonably, "I have decided that the simplest way out of
this business is for you to die" (p. 209). The grenade is for the
congressman to kill himself with; he does. "He had annoyed me,"
Wolfe complains with a touch of pique at the end. "He had chal-
lenged me" (p. 219).

The Doorbell Rang (1965) offers Wolfe what the dust jacket
terms "his toughest opponent ever"—the Federal Bureau of Investigation. Mrs. Rachel Bruner, who has incurred the agency's
wrath by mailing out ten thousand free copies of *The F.B.I. Nobody Knows*, hires the fat man "to do something that perhaps no
other man alive could do" (p. 5).[47] Explains Mrs. Bruner:

"I am being followed day and night. I believe 'tailed' is the
word. So is my son, and my daughter, and my secretary, and
my brother. My telephones are tapped, and my son thinks his
is. . . . My lawyers say there is probably no way to stop it,
but they are considering it. They are one of the biggest and

best firms in New York, and even *they* are afraid of the FBI!"
(pp. 6–7)

She offers Wolfe $100,000 to put a stop to it all. Archie's view of
the FBI is at least as respectful—and suspicious—as that of Mrs.
Bruner's lawyers:

[If we took the case,] whenever I left the house I'd spend all
my time ditching tails, and good ones. . . . Our phone would
be tapped. . . . They might or might not try a frame. . . .
Windows and doors, even one with a chain bolt, are pie for
them. They could monitor our mail. . . . They have six
thousand trained men, some of them as good as they come,
and three hundred million dollars a year. (p. 18)

Naturally, Wolfe takes the case.

The vision of the FBI in action is sufficiently nightmarish.
"Modern science was fixing it so nobody can know what the hell
is going on," Goodwin complains (p. 42). Modern science has further fixed it so nobody knows what the FBI is up to. The assumption has to be that they're listening in: Archie and his boss are
reduced to talking before a blaring television in the basement to
obviate transmission. When Wolfe asks if they can be overheard,
his lieutenant shrugs:

"I don't know. I've read about a thing that is supposed to
pick up voices half a mile off, but I don't know about how
much area it covers or about obstructions like walls and floors.
There could be items I haven't heard about that can take a
whole house. If there aren't there soon will be. People will
have to talk with their hands." (p. 87)

Inspector Cramer is at hand again, chafing over an unsolved murder that he cannot pursue because three special agents were seen
leaving the scene of the crime. The dead man had been an author
collecting material for an FBI exposé; the material left the premises with the agents. No one is incapable of surmising that the
defunct scribe fell victim to a federal gun.

Wolfe uses the crime as a lever against the agency. His presence alone is enough to get the government to attempt a revocation of his license. The fault does not ostensibly lie with Wolfe; Archie emphasizes his chief's motives are pure: "If the right to make security checks is being abused so that the personal or property rights of citizens are being violated, that isn't a private matter" (p. 34). But Goodwin's tactics are at least as curious as his adversary's: in seeking evidence against unauthorized FBI entry, he openly proceeds to (what else?) commit burglary.

> "I was clean until I stood at Sarah Dacos's door and got out the collection of keys. When I had knocked twice, and pushed the button twice and heard the ring, with no response, I tried a key. The fourth one did it, smooth and easy. I put the [rubber] gloves on, turned the knob, opened the door, crossed the sill, and shut the door, and I had broken and entered according to the statutes of the State of New York." (p. 133)

Wolfe and Goodwin then trap two agents in an illegal sneak into their own premises. Wolfe promptly blackmails the bureau into laying off Mrs. Bruner unless they want the break-in publicized.

It unfolds that the FBI, besides removing the author's papers from his rooms, also removed the bullet that killed him. By the end of the novel, Wolfe has discovered the culprit (it has taken him a whole week) and succeeded in manipulating his own outlawry and that of the FBI and the New York City Police Department in making arrangements for the killer's prosecution. Special Agent Wragg delivers the stolen bullet to Inspector Cramer, disavowing any knowledge of it thereafter; Cramer prepares to have one of his officers perjure himself in testimony on how the bullet was uncovered; and Messrs. Wolfe and Goodwin get away with breaking and entering, withholding and tampering with evidence. Justice then prevails, as it might have if everybody had behaved themselves in the first place. At the novel's close the boss of the FBI himself is left alone on Wolfe's doorstep to turn slowly, slowly in the wind.

In the introduction to his edition of *The Great Detective Stories* (1927), Willard Huntington Wright noted that most of the stories he had collected were written by English authors. He argued that "the English novelist takes this type of fiction more seriously than we do." [48] What he meant was that the riddle story, presided over by the aesthete-intellectual, had not progressed in America as it had in England under the able craftsmanship of writers like Agatha Christie (*The Mysterious Affair at Styles*, 1920), Dorothy Sayers (*Whose Body?*, 1923), and E. C. Bentley (*Trent's Last Case*, 1930); but something else had developed in its stead. A new kind of detective story, emphasizing character and scene rather than esoterica, was being written in the United States, and it was taken very seriously indeed by its practitioners. This new kind of detective story had a new kind of detective—a working man, who pursued crime not as a hobby but for a living. If Philo Vance was "a man of unusual culture and brilliance," [49] the new detective was fairly ordinary, though streetwise; if Vance was "an aristocrat by birth and instinct," the new detective was unregenerately a commoner with common tastes and common sympathies. The Pinkerton man now supplanted Vidocq. But he and Vance yet shared one common trait: the assumption that the law is individually interpretable and personally executable.

The primitive early version of the working private cop was Nick Carter; although he served as consultant to a customarily confounded police, he fought the forces of the ungodly because, as he expressed it, "That is the profession I have followed." [50] Dime novel veteran of more than a thousand titles published between the late 1800s and the 1920s, Carter appeared first in "The Old Detective's Pupil; or, The Mysterious Crime of Madison Square," a novelette in Street and Smith's *New York Weekly* for September 18, 1886. John Coryell was the author; he later surrendered his interest in the tales to Frederick Marmaduke Van Rensselaer Dey, who wrote a Carter story a week for seventeen years. At 25,000 words a story, Dey produced four to five thousand words daily— with the help of perhaps a dozen other writers—before he shot himself in a cheap hotel in 1922. [51] Dey's character, as Robert Clurman notes, had the personality of a Pinkerton: "Nick had no vices. He did not drink, smoke or swear and he never shaded the truth save when he was trying to outwit some culprit, at which time, of course, no holds were barred. Dey once said that he 'never wrote a Nick Carter story that he wouldn't read to a Bible class.' " [52]

The first Dey effort was "Nick Carter, Detective; by a Celebrated Author" (1891), and just as Nick's character owes itself to Pinkerton, so the plot belongs to Poe. Like "The Murders in the Rue Morgue," the story concerns itself with the locked-room murder of a woman committed by a loose pet—this time a python. The owner of the snake is a strangler who learned the trade from the Indian Thug cult ("Oh, how I love to see them gasp for breath"). [53] It is the strangler's habit to carry a cobra around with him in his watch pocket; Nick subdues both by striking down the one and shooting the other. Observes the police chief admiringly: "That was a remarkable shot with no light but the flaring torch of a peanut stand." [54]

Another entry in the series is "Nick Carter and the Professor; or, Solving a Scientific Problem" (1902), in which "the little giant" and his assistant Chickering Carter (mercifully shortened to "Chick") search out grave robbers and an addled scientist who employs "solvents" to restore the dead to life. The scientist unsurprisingly fails at this. After being assaulted variously and lassoed from a moving automobile, Nick tracks his foe to an operating room where Professor Drummond is about to continue his experiments on an eighteen-year-old girl. When Carter intervenes, Drummond attempts suicide. As Chick moves to stop him, Carter responds with sentiments that should especially disturb a Van Rennsselaer Dey Bible class: " 'Let him go, Chick,' said Nick hurriedly. 'It is simply a dangerous lunatic out of the way. We must save better lives. . . .' " [55] Carter may embody, in Clurman's terms, "the notions of goodness, probity, daring and courage of a relatively uncomplicated time," [56] but he also reveals a curious selectivity about the value of human life.

The descendants of Dupin and Holmes, all of them bizarre, were representative of the faith of their time in the ultimate resourcefulness of the human mind. They were bizarre because the popular mind of that time conceived eccentricity to be closely allied to genius; since genius was capable of all things, it could be indulged its affectations. Allied to genius, affectation was endearing rather than tiresome. This attitude could not and did not last. World war, nationwide depression, high-level failures both diplomatic and economic—these called to serious question the faith that assured everyone there was a way out of it all if the best brains just sat down and went to work. The best brains had already brought disaster in the name of progress; the Theory of Relativity now implied the insignificance of the human mind, not its grandeur. American anti-intellectualism, deploring the aesthete because he smacked of that aristocracy that wars and revolutions had been fought to depose, had been vindicated: in pursuit of evil, brains were insufficient. What was needed more was muscle. Russell Nye observes that

> the society in which Vance, [Ellery] Queen, and even Charlie Chan operated was an essentially rational world in which crime could be solved by the man of logic. Postwar society was different. In a world of paid-off cops, corrupt politicians, rich crooks, expensive call girls, and contract murder, logic did not necessarily work. The question of who put the weed-killer in Aunt Hetty's bouillon was of little interest compared to that of who would (or could) break the power of the gangster czar.[57]

So what came to be called the "hard-boiled" hero began like Nick Carter to take on the characteristics of the athlete and discard those of the artist. He combined the tenuous respectability of Vidocq with the Puritan rectitude of Pinkerton: he had been around, but he still *believed*. Those who had come before him rejected women partly because they represented an intuitive principle that had no place in the scientific method and partly because romance interfered with reason. Now the private eye would acquire glands, if not a heart.

NOTES

1. John Philip Stead, *Vidocq: A Biography* (New York: Ray Publishers, 1954), p. 10.
2. Stead, p. 21.
3. Stead, pp. 105–6.
4. Stead, p. 125.
5. Eugène-François Vidocq, *Vidocq: The Personal Memoirs of the First Great Detective*, trans. and ed. Edwin Gile Rich (Cambridge, Mass.: Riverside Press, 1935), p. viii.
6. Stead, p. 161.

7. James D. Horan, *The Pinkertons: The Detective Dynasty That Made History* (New York: Crown, 1967), p. 20.

8. Horan, p. 25.

9. Horan, p. 26.

10. Allan Pinkerton, *History and Evidence of the Passage of Abraham Lincoln from Harrisburg, Pa., to Washington, D.C., on the Twenty-third of February, Eighteen hundred and sixty-one* [U.S.A.] n.d., n.p. See also Norma B. Cuthbert, ed., *Lincoln and the Baltimore Plot 1861: From Pinkerton Records and Related Papers* (San Marino, Calif.: Huntington Library, 1949).

11. Horan, p. 201.

12. Citations to Pinkerton's *The Expressman and the Detective* are from the W. B. Keen, Cooke edition (Chicago, 1875).

13. Citations to Pinkerton's *The Molly Maguires and the Detectives* are from the G. W. Dillingham reprint of the 1877 edition (New York, 1905).

14. Richard Wilmer Rowan, *The Pinkertons: A Detective Dynasty* (Boston: Little, Brown, 1931), p. 270.

15. Robert A. W. Lowndes, "The Contributions of Edgar Allan Poe," in *The Mystery Writer's Art,* ed. Francis M. Nevins, Jr. (Bowling Green, Ohio: Bowling Green University Popular Press, 1970), p. 2.

16. Citations to Poe's "The Murders in the Rue Morgue" are from *The Complete Works of Edgar Allan Poe,* ed. James A. Harrison (New York: AMS Press, 1965), III, 146–92.

17. John Walsh, *Poe the Detective: The Curious Circumstances Behind "The Mystery of Marie Rogêt"* (New Brunswick, N.J.: Rutgers University Press, 1968).

18. Edgar Allan Poe, "The Mystery of Marie Rogêt," in *The Complete Works of Edgar Allan Poe,* ed. James A. Harrison (New York: AMS Press, 1965), IV, 8.

19. Citations to Poe's "The Purloined Letter" are from *The Complete Works of Edgar Allan Poe,* ed. James A. Harrison (New York: AMS Press, 1965), VI, 28–52.

20. Citations to Doyle are from *The Complete Sherlock Holmes* (Garden City, N.Y.: Doubleday, Doran, 1930).

21. William S. Baring-Gould, "Two Doctors and a Detective: Sir Arthur Conan Doyle, John H. Watson, M.D., and Mr. Sherlock Holmes of Baker Street," in *The Annotated Sherlock Holmes* (New York: Clarkson N. Potter, 1967), I, 12.

22. Baring-Gould, I, 17.

23. Baring-Gould, I, 14–17.

24. Willard Huntington Wright, "The Detective Story," in *The*

Great Detective Stories: A Chronological Anthology (New York: Scribner's, 1927), pp. 9–10.

25. S. S. Van Dine [Willard Huntington Wright], *The Greene Murder Case* (New York: Scribner's, 1927), p. 4; hereafter cited as *Greene.*

26. S. S. Van Dine, *The Benson Murder Case* (New York: Scribner's, 1926), pp. 6–7; hereafter cited as *Benson.*

27. *Greene*, p. 8.

28. *Greene*, p. 22.

29. *Benson*, pp. 12–13.

30. *Benson*, p. 107.

31. *Benson*, p. 72.

32. *Benson*, p. 76.

33. *Greene*, p. 126.

34. *Benson*, p. 336.

35. *Greene*, p. 90.

36. S. S. Van Dine [Willard Huntington Wright], *The Bishop Murder Case* (New York: Scribner's, 1929), p. 313; hereafter cited as *Bishop.*

37. *Bishop*, pp. 348–49.

38. *Benson*, p. 115.

39. William S. Baring-Gould, *Sherlock Holmes of Baker Street: The Life of the World's First Consulting Detective* (New York: Clarkson N. Potter, 1962), p. 212. See also William S. Baring-Gould, *Nero Wolfe of West Thirty-Fifth Street* (New York: Viking Press, 1969).

40. Rex Stout, *Fer-de-Lance* (New York: Farrar and Rinehart, 1934), p. 100; hereafter cited as *Fer-de-Lance.*

41. Rex Stout, "Not Quite Dead Enough," in *Not Quite Dead Enough* (New York: Farrar and Rinehart, 1942), p. 10.

42. *Fer-de-Lance,* p. 5.

43. "Not Quite Dead Enough," p. 5.

44. Rex Stout, *The Doorbell Rang* (New York: Viking Press, 1965), p. 94.

45. Subsequent citations to Stout's *Fer-de-Lance* are from the Farrar and Rinehart edition (New York, 1934).

46. Citations to Stout's "Booby Trap" are from *Not Quite Dead Enough* (New York: Farrar and Rinehart, 1942), pp. 109–220.

47. Subsequent citations to Stout's *The Doorbell Rang* are from the Viking Press edition (New York, 1965).

48. Wright, p. 29.

49. *Benson*, p. 9.

50. Quoted in Russel Nye, *The Unembarrassed Muse: The Popular Arts in America* (New York: Dial Press, 1970), p. 209.

51. Robert Clurman, Introduction to *Nick Carter, Detective: The*

Adventures of Fiction's Most Celebrated Detective, Anon. (New York: Dell, 1963), pp. 7–9.

52. Clurman, p. 10.

53. Frederick Dey, "Nick Carter, Detective," in *Nick Carter, Detective: The Adventures of Fiction's Most Celebrated Detective,* Anon. (New York: Dell, 1963), p. 36.

54. Dey, p. 55.

55. Anon., "Nick Carter and the Professor; or, Solving a Scientific Problem," in *Nick Carter, Detective: The Adventures of Fiction's Most Celebrated Detective* (New York: Dell, 1963), p. 316.

56. Clurman, p. 12.

57. Nye, p. 257.

THREE. The Kid from Cyanide Gulch

"I haven't laughed so much since the hogs ate my kid brother."
—The Continental Op

The hard-boiled detective was a product of the action pulp magazine industry that spread itself across the United States during the 1920s and 1930s. So called because of its woodpulp origin, the newsstand pulp was a cheap paper anthology that took the place of the popular dime novel and eventually existed in more than two hundred versions of detective, Western, science fiction, and romance monthlies.[1]

The pulp called *Black Mask* (now subsumed into *Ellery Queen's Mystery Magazine*) most particularly provided the private eye. Accruing immediately a circulation that spanned the United States, Canada, and Great Britain, the magazine with the eyemask logo was counted quality by reader and writer alike: pulp veteran Frank Gruber, creator of Simon Lash and Shotgun Slade, referred to it wistfully as "the Ace of Aces, the goal of all pulp writers. . . . The elite of the elite were the *Black Mask* writers."[2] In order to fund their less successful *Smart Set*, H. L. Mencken and George Jean Nathan founded *Black Mask* in 1920.[3] The clipped dialogue and narrative drive of the stories they printed became a trademark and influenced the entire industry. Writer and pulp collector Ron Goulart records the magazine's success:

> The new kind of American detective story pioneered by *Black Mask* caught on. The hardboiled trend spread to such pulp magazines as *Detective Fiction Weekly* and Street and Smith's *Detective Story*. Machine guns, tough guys, .45 automatics, hoodlums, cops and cons blossomed on the covers of the pulps. The bandwagon, black and low slung, began to roll and the 30's saw more and more magazines getting into the detective business. Now on the stands were *Action Detective, Greater Gangster Stories, Dime Detective, Nickel Detective, Black Aces, Black Book Detective, Triple Detective, Strange Detective, Gang Worlds, Thrilling Detective, Crime Busters, Spicy Detective* and *New Detective*.[4]

Under the editorship of George W. Sutton, Jr., and later Joseph Thompson Shaw, *Black Mask* demanded character in conjunction with action set down in prose that could be called poetry with nails in it. The *Black Mask* "stable" boasted the best in the business. Along with Gruber (*The French Key; Simon Lash, Private Detective*) were Peter Uric, writing as "Paul Cain" (*Fast One*); Frederick Nebel (*Sleepers East, Six Deadly Dames*); Raoul Whitfield (*Death in a Bowl, Green Ice*); Erle Stanley Gardner (*The Case of the Velvet Claws, Owls Don't Blink*); Horace McCoy (*They Shoot Horses, Don't They?; Kiss Tomorrow Goodbye*); and Lester Dent (*Dead at the Takeoff, Lady Afraid*), who as "Kenneth Robeson" wrote the Doc Savage stories. Sutton's seminal find, however, was Carroll John Daly (*The Snarl of the Beast, The Hidden Hand*), who in Race Williams created the prototype for the modern private eye.

Daly was an ex-usher and assistant theater manager with aspirations to become an actor. In a sense he fulfilled them, for although he was a slight man whose phobias kept him from going to the dentist,[5] his creation was as tough as they come. The .45-packing Williams called himself "a middleman—just a halfway house between the cops and the crooks. . . . I do a little honest shooting once in a while—just in the way of business [but] I never bumped off a guy what didn't need it." [6] Williams explained once: "Many people have their little peculiarities. Mine was holding a loaded gun in my hand while I sleep." [7] Although he announced "I'm all for justice and fair play," [8] justice and fair play for Williams resided well beyond the law. "Right and wrong are not written on the statutes for me, nor do I find my code of morals in the essays of long-winded professors. My ethics are my own." [9] So a typical Williams story could end like this: "I sent him crashing through the gates of hell with my bullet in his brain." [10]

The rag-thief writing of Daly was soon supplanted by the terse musical argot of Samuel Dashiell Hammett, an ex-Pinkerton man whose work was so promoted by editor Shaw that Erle Stanley Gardner (later the creator of popular lawyer-detective Perry Mason) accused him of trying to "Hammetize" *Black Mask*. "Shaw not only went all out for Hammett," wrote Gardner, "but tried to get writers to follow the Hammett style." [11] Frank Gruber noted that style was as essential as substance to the *Black Mask* editorship: "At its best, *Black Mask* published the sparsest prose of any magazine in the country. Joe Shaw used to admonish his new writers, 'Prune and cut, don't use a single word that you can do without.' " [12] Captain Shaw, winner of the national championship in sabre and the president's medal for championship in epée, foil, and sabre,[13] an innovator said to have perfected an epée stroke against which there was no defense,[14] believed as a swordsman in the unity of form and expression; as a swordsman, too, he believed in a certain economy of gesture, a paring away of superfluous motion. Thus the crisp cadences of Hammett became a standard for Shaw and anybody else interested in the admirable articulation of unspeakable things. As Philip Durham expressed it, "Hammett went into the American alleys and came out with an authentic expression of the people who live in and by violence." [15]

Dashiell Hammett knew something about detectives. As a Pinkerton agent in Baltimore and later in San Francisco he had traveled widely and handled criminal matters ranging from international gold smuggling to the theft of a Ferris wheel. Hammett took part in the tracking of silk-pajama gambler Nicky Arnstein, Fanny Brice's horse-fancier—and bond-thief—husband. He had been in on the investigation of the rape case that cost film comedian Fatty Arbuckle his career (Hammett pronounced it a newspaper "frame-up" [16]). The victim of tuberculosis and heavy drinking, Hammett left his wife and child in a serious effort to become a writer; in 1923, based upon his own agency experience, he created the Continental Op.

The nameless Op appeared in thirty-six stories written over seven years, most of them printed in *Black Mask;* eight were revised into two Op novels. The Op, who admits "I've got horny skin all over what's left of my soul" (p. 36),[17] is fat, forty, and not inclined toward affectation (qualities which may carry some surprise for those who celebrated William Conrad's 1971 television series *Cannon* as an innovation). "The idea in this detective business is to catch crooks, not to put on heroics," proclaims the Op.[18] He works for the Continental Detective Agency, a crypto-Pinkerton firm, and his Pinkerton personality is based upon that of Hammett's superior, James Wright, assistant superintendent of Pinkerton's Baltimore office.[19] In spite of his implacably enlisted attitude, the Op has held a captain's commission in the wartime military intelligence department and speaks French and German (pp. 115–72).

Hammett's private detective is an organization man whose ingrained procedural sense developed from years of dangerous routine lends the kind of confidence that comes from simply surviving that routine for so long. Confronting oversized opposition in "The Whosis Kid" (1925), the Op reflects that he has "been in too many rumpuses to mind them much. Usually nothing very bad happens to you, even if you lose. I wasn't going to back down just because this big stiff was meatier than I." [20]

"Few men get killed," he explains later. "Most of those who meet sudden ends *get themselves* killed. I've had twenty years of experience at dodging that." [21] The tough professionalism of the Op is the expressionless reaction to the clowning of the dilettante detective of the English school. Fat rather than photogenic, unsporting in the extreme, this is one detective absolutely uninterested in Oriental porcelain or anything else unconnected with his work. He does not study Egyptology; he does not grow orchids. "My face doesn't scare children," he admits, "but it's a more or less truthful witness to a life that hasn't been overwhelmed with refinement and gentility" (p. 399). He has no sedulous associate to tell his story for him, chain-smokes Fatimas instead of rose-tipped *Régies,* and offers no alibis for his ruthlessness—because the ruthlessness is necessary. Having cornered roughneck Babe McCloor in "Fly Paper" (1929), the Op levels his gun and demands surrender.

> "I'm no Annie Oakley, but if I can't pop your kneecaps with two shots at this distance, you're welcome to me. And if you think smashed kneecaps are a lot of fun, give it a whirl."
> "Hell with that," he said and charged.
> I shot him in the right knee.
> He lurched toward me.
> I shot his left knee.
> He tumbled down.
> "You would have it," I complained. (p. 68)

This kind of terseness is typical of the Hammett pro, who wastes neither words nor pity on the opposition. As conman Paddy the Mex once observed, "This little fat guy will do anything for anybody, if only he can send 'em over for life in the end" (p. 353).

The Op's boss is as anonymous as his agent. A kind of loveless deity known only as the Old Man, as San Francisco bureau chief he is a personification of his subordinate's future; it is easy to imagine the fat detective graduating to a level of emotionlessness only slightly removed from his own and becoming himself "the Old Man, with his gentle eyes behind gold spectacles and his mild smile, hiding the fact that fifty years of sleuthing had left him without any feelings at all on any subject" (p. 91). The obverse of inferential Sherlock Holmes, he is "one of those cautious babies who'll look out of the window at a cloudburst and say, 'It seems to be raining,' on the off-chance that somebody's pouring water off the roof" (p. 364). There is nothing at all endearing, however, about this gray, passionless man, and the admiration he receives from the Op has nothing filial in it. "We who worked under him were proud of his cold-bloodedness. We used to boast he could spit icicles in July, and we called him Pontius Pilate among ourselves, because he smiled politely when he sent us out to be crucified on suicidal jobs" (p. 359). The Old Man is the apotheosis of professionalism, the mechanically efficient automaton the Op seems bent on becoming. The Op stories are the chronicle of that evolution.

What there is of the Op's heart is never permitted to interfere with what he is supposed to do. Conducting the painful interrogation of a fresh suicide's husband in "The Scorched Face" (1925), the Op ruminates typically: "I felt sorry for him, but I had work to do" (p. 82). In "The Gutting of Couffignal" (1925), he explains to a lady captive why he can't be bribed to let her go:

"Now I'm a detective because I happen to like the work. It pays me a fair salary, but I could find other jobs that could pay more. Even a hundred dollars more a month would be twelve hundred a year. Say twenty-five or thirty thousand dollars in the years between now and my sixtieth birthday.

"Now I pass up about twenty-five or thirty thousand of honest gain because I like being a detective, like the work.

And liking the work makes you want to do it as well as you can. Otherwise there'd be no sense to it. That's the fix I am in. I don't know anything else, don't want to know or enjoy anything else. You can't weigh that against any sum of money. Money is good stuff. I haven't anything against it. But in the past eighteen years I've been getting my fun out of chasing crooks and tackling puzzles, my satisfaction out of catching crooks and solving riddles. It's the only kind of sport I know anything about, and I can't imagine a pleasanter future than twenty-some more years of it." (p. 34)

The lady responds that her offer includes a great deal more than money. The Op leans on a crutch he has taken from a one-legged boy in his pursuit of her and shakes his head. "You think I'm a man and you're a woman. That's wrong. I'm a manhunter and you're something that has been running in front of me. There's nothing human about it" (p. 34). The woman refuses to believe he'll shoot her and walks out on him. So he shoots her. "You ought to have known I'd do it!" he growls. "Didn't I steal a crutch from a cripple?" (p. 38).

The signs of sadism in the Op are only the inevitable evidence of what happens to a man whose engagement in his work is unconnected with any human empathy. "I'm only a hired man with a hired man's interest in your troubles," he explains.[22] And he gets his "fun" in a fashion that is often frenetic: "I laughed in his purple face and brought my own hands up. Each of them picked one of his little fingers out of my flesh. . . . I twisted them back. They broke together." [23] Waiting to bash the bad guy with a lead pipe, the Op pauses to wonder if "I was now enjoying the rewards of my virtue—in a heaven where I could enjoy myself forever and ever socking folks who had been rough with me down below" (p. 407). The Op is a man who relishes roughhouse; in "The Big Knockover" (1927) he becomes Achilles of the alleys in a saloon fight:

A squint-eyed Portuguese slashed at my neck with a knife that spoiled my necktie. I caught him over the ear with the side of my gun before he got away, saw the ear tear loose. A grinning kid of twenty went down for my legs—football stuff.

I felt his teeth in the knee I pumped up, and felt them break. A pock-marked mulatto pushed a gunbarrel over the shoulder of the man in front of him. My blackjack crunched the arm of the man in front. He winced sidewise as the mulatto pulled the trigger—and had the side óf his face blown away.

I fired twice—once when a gun was leveled within a foot of my middle, once when I discovered a man standing on a table not far off taking careful aim at my head. For the rest I trusted to my arms and legs, and saved bullets. The night was young and I had only a dozen pills—six in the gun, six in my pocket.

It was a swell bag of nails. Swing right, swing left, kick, swing right, swing left, kick. Don't hesitate, don't look for targets. God will see that there's always a mug there for your gun or blackjack to sock, a belly for your foot. (p. 388)

The Op seems to like this part of his job too much. When he poses as a thug, the fat man does not really seem to lose his identity at all; he rather confirms it. His humor is graveyard stuff, often making fun of his incapacity for feeling, as in this scene from the same story in which Big Flora works over wounded Red O'Leary:

I stood beside Flora, smoking cigarettes from the pack she had given me. When she raised her head, I would transfer the cigarette from my mouth to hers. . . .

Her bare arms were blood to the elbows. Her face was damp with sweat. It was a gory mess, and it took time. But when she straightened up for the last smoke, the bullet was out of Red, the bleeding had stopped, and he was bandaged.

"Thank God that's over," I said, lighting one of my own cigarettes. "These pills you smoke are terrible." (p. 398)

But the most disturbing side of the Op's nature is how much he is willing to sacrifice for the job. He is quite capable of marshaling the powers of life and death simply to save Continental a scandal, and whatever guilt he feels about it is insufficient to interfere with his rest. In "$106,000 Blood Money" (1927), Continental's finest is after a hoodlum boss named Papadopoulos who specializes in double-crossing his confreres. When the Op realizes fellow agent Jack Counihan has cooperated with the Greek, he sets him up for a kill and admits, sourly, "I'm another Papadopoulos" (p. 455). When he confronts the Old Man with the event, he realizes that such is their mutual professional instinct that nothing really needs to be said about it.

> I knew what he was thinking. He was thinking that if Jack had come through alive we would have had the nasty choice between letting him go free or giving the Agency a black eye by advertising the fact that one of our operatives was a crook.
> I threw my cigarette away and stood up. The Old Man stood also, and held a hand out to me.
> "Thanks," he said. (p. 458) [24]

The Op has had a man taken off, but for the good of the firm—in the manner of a syndicate hit man.

This reading makes it difficult to agree with Philip Durham that *Black Mask* heroes like Race Williams and the Continental Op "were violent, but their violence was not merely that of sensationalism. It was rather a kind of meaningful violence, sometimes symbolic of a special ethical code or attitude, sometimes an explicit description and implicit criticism of a corrupt society." [25] The significance of the "ethical code" of the Op is that it is so fundamentally ambiguous; the Op does not resist bribery because it is wrong but because it is unprofessional, and his moral sense confines itself to what either gets the job done or benefits the agency. "Meaningful violence" is a hard term to untangle, but if is suggestive of any justification for the Op's brutality it attempts to elevate him to a kind of knighthood Hammett never intended for him. The violence of the Op's world *is* a criticism of a corrupt society—but the corruption now includes the Op, and it is a society in which heroes are cutthroats who use enemy tactics to clean up the town. And the town will not stay clean.

But *Black Mask,* and particularly Hammett, were responsible for the establishment of a concrete, no-nonsense style that might be called reportorial lyricism. Hammett's bleak catalog of the dead in a Fillmore Street massacre clearly expresses his ear for both the rhythms of colloquial speech and the repetitive cadence of consonantal sound:

> There was the Dis-and-Dat Kid, who had crashed out of Leavenworth only two months before; Sheeny Holmes; Snohomish Shitey, supposed to have died a hero in France in 1919; L. A. Slim, from Denver, sockless and underwearless as usual, with a thousand-dollar bill sewed in each shoulder of his coat; Spider Girucci wearing a steel-mesh vest under his shirt and a scar from crown to chin where his brother carved him years ago; Old Pete Best, once a congressman; Nigger Vojan, who once won $175,000 in a Chicago crapgame—*Abracadabra* tattooed on him in three places; Alphabet Shorty McCoy; Tom Brooks, Alphabet Shorty's brother-in-law, who invented the Richmond razzle-dazzle and bought three hotels with the profits; Red Cudahy, who stuck up a Union Pacific train in 1924; Denny Burke; Bull McGonickle, still pale from fifteen years in Joliet; Toby the Lugs, Bull's running-mate, who used to brag about picking President Wilson's pocket in a Washington vaudeville theatre; and Paddy the Mex. (p. 372)

A reasonable guess would be that this passage influenced Fitzgerald's famous description of the guests in chapter 4 of *The Great Gatsby;* but Hammett influenced others as well. As Kenneth Millar wrote in his essay on the writer as detective hero, "the *Black Mask* revolution was a real one. From it emerged a new kind of detective hero, the classless, restless men of American democracy, who spoke the language of the street." [26] The Op stories are the first American detective stories that might genuinely be called literature, and they do not date, largely because the dehumanized Op achieves victories that are, given his world, at best short-term. This kind of antihero, made brutal by situations that demand it of him, finds sympathy in a country increasingly suspicious of the grand gesture and in a century in which the truly flamboyant figure, *à la* Patton or T. E. Lawrence, has often been deranged. The Op does not surpass his time, he expresses it.

Hammett's first novel, *Red Harvest* (1929), is a picture of the

Op berserk. It is the story of how the fat man enters a malign realm
and leaves it, touching and being touched by what he encounters.
It is not, as Robert Brown Parker has written, an account of the
Op's total "commitment against the forces of evil"; [27] and if, as
George J. Thompson III has written, "the Op has vowed to clean
up a community, to act as scourge," it is difficult to agree with his
assertion that "we approve." [28] We are not intended to. For in this
novel the Op abandons rather than adheres to his professionalism
in taking on the role of avenging angel.

The Op had received a letter from newspaper publisher Donald
Willsson to come to Personville "to do some work for him" (p.
10).[29] Personville, like the Pottsville of Allan Pinkerton's *Molly
Maguires and the Detectives,* is a fallen Eden now popularly
dubbed "Poisonville."

> The city wasn't pretty. Most of its builders had gone in for
> gaudiness. Maybe they had been successful at first. Since
> then the smelters whose brick stacks stuck up tall against a
> gloomy mountain to the south had yellow-smoked everything
> into uniform dinginess. The result was an ugly city of forty
> thousand people, set in an ugly notch between two ugly
> mountains that had been all dirtied up by mining. Spread
> over this was a grimy sky that looked as if it had come out of
> the smelter's stacks. (p. 3)

The law in Personville has an unkempt look on the Op's arrival:
"The first policeman I saw needed a shave. The second had a
couple of buttons off his shabby uniform. The third stood in the
center of the city's main intersection—Broadway and Union
Streets—directing traffic, with a cigar in one corner of his mouth"
(p. 3). This appearance of decay and ineptitude is quickly borne
out by the murder of Willsson before the Op has time to see him.
The Op discovers Willsson's father, Elihu, owns the town "heart,
soul, skin and guts." He learns further that the elder Willsson's
control has slipped to the thugs he has hired over the years to do
his "bleeding" for him (p. 7). After the Op decides to find out
who killed the son, Elihu hires him "to smoke out the rats" (p.
29). The Op takes the assignment, but makes certain demands
of his own. "I'd have to have a free hand," he warns, "no favors

to anybody—run the job as I pleased." He insists that the old manipulator settle for "a complete job or nothing" (p. 30). And then the fun begins.

What ensues is the story of how the Op's mission changes from a professional one to a personal one as he becomes corrupted by the corrupt world in which he finds himself. At the beginning of the novel he is able to say, "When I say *me,* I mean the Continental" (p. 30). By the latter part of the book he is falsifying his reports ("It's right enough for the Agency to have rules and regulations, but when you're out on a job you've got to do it the best way you can" [p. 78]) and lying to the Old Man. He no longer is Continental's unmoved extension; he is his own man, having achieved an identity through violence. What has begun as a job of work ends up a vendetta, and the Op becomes less and less sure of his motives as the story proceeds.

In going after the ungodly, among whom are assorted bosses, thugs, and a chief of police, Hammett's hero plays one side off the other in the manner of his film heir, Sergio Leone's "Man with No Name" in *A Fistful of Dollars.* Like the impassive Clint Eastwood character, the emotionless Op does not play gently. In one scene he murders a cop to convince the mob he has no allegiances there; in another he is responsible for the knifing of a prizefighter whom he has blackmailed into refusing to throw a fight. When Willsson tries to call him off the case, the Op refuses. He is no longer a hired man, but a free agent with a grudge.

> "Your fat chief of police tried to assassinate me last night. I don't like that. I'm just mean enough to want to ruin him for it. Now I'm going to have my fun. I've got ten thousand dollars of your money to play with. I'm going to use it opening Poisonville up from Adam's apple to ankles." (p. 43)

Which he does. But not as a hired man; his client has withdrawn. "I don't like the way Poisonville has treated me," he complains. "I've got my chance now, and I'm going to even up" (p. 45).

Bodies pile up. The Op calls in two more Continental detectives, Dick Foley and Mickey Linehan, to help him. "If we can smash things up enough—break the combination—they'll have their knives in each other's backs, doing our work for us," he tells them (p. 78). "But there's no use taking anybody into court, no matter what you've got on them. They own the courts, and, besides, the courts are too slow for us now" (p. 79). More bodies pile up. The Op admits on receiving a telegram from the Old Man that "to have sent him the dope he wanted at that time would have been the same as sending in my resignation" (p. 95). He's neck deep in Poisonville and by now poisoned by it; he won't be the same afterward. "Everybody's killing everybody," groans the police chief, sick of it all (p. 95), and the Op promptly sets him up to be shot. At length Continental's man admits things are happening to him: "I've arranged a killing or two in my time, when they were necessary. But this is the first time I ever got the fever. It's this damned burg. You can't go straight here" (p. 102). He muses further, "Play with murder enough, and it gets you one of two ways. It makes you sick, or you get to like it" (p. 102). The way it has gotten the Op is clear. He admits he could have swung "the play legally. I could have done that. But it's easier to have them killed off, easier and surer, and, now that I'm feeling this way, more satisfying" (p. 104). He has gone "blood-simple, like the natives" (p. 102).

In the course of things the Op passes out under gin and laudanum in a prostitute's living room and has two dreams. They are worth quoting at length. The first deals with a woman:

> I dreamed I was sitting on a bench, in Baltimore, facing the tumbling fountain in Harlem Park, beside a woman who wore a veil. I had come there with her. She was somebody I knew well. But I had suddenly forgotten who she was. I couldn't see her face because of the long black veil.
>
> I thought that if I said something to her I would recognize her voice when she answered. But I was very embarrassed and was a long time finding anything to say. Finally I asked her if she knew a man named Carroll T. Harris.
>
> She answered me, but the roar and swish of the tumbling fountain smothered her voice, and I could hear nothing.
>
> Fire engines went out Edmondson Avenue. She left me to run after them. As she ran she cried, "Fire! Fire!" I recognized her voice then and knew who she was, and ran after her, but it was too late. She and the fire engines were gone.

I walked the streets hunting for her, half the streets in the United States, Gay Street and Mount Royal Avenue in Baltimore, Colfax Avenue in Denver, Aetna Road and St. Clair Avenue in Cleveland, McKinney Avenue in Dallas, Lemartine and Cornell and Amory Streets in Boston, Berry Boulevard in Louisville, Lexington Avenue in New York, until I came to Victoria Street in. Jacksonville, where I heard her voice again, though I still could not see her.

I walked more streets, listening to her voice. She was calling a name, not mine, one strange to me, but no matter how fast I walked or in what direction, I could get no nearer her voice. It was the same distance from me in the street that runs past the Federal Building in El Paso as in Detroit's Grand Circus Park. Then the voice stopped.

Tired and discouraged, I went into the lobby of the hotel that faces the railroad station in Rocky Mount, North Carolina, to rest. While I sat there a train came in. She got off it and came into the lobby, over to me, and began kissing me. I was very uncomfortable because everybody stood around looking at us and laughing. (p. 107)

The second dream concerns a man:

I dreamed I was in a strange city hunting for a man I hated. I had an open knife in my pocket and meant to kill him with it when I found him. It was Sunday morning. Church bells were ringing, crowds of people were in the streets, going to and from church. I walked almost as far as in the first dream, but always in the same strange city.

Then the man I was after yelled at me, and I saw him. He was a small brown man who wore an immense sombrero. He was standing on the steps of a tall building on the far side of a wide plaza, laughing at me. Between us, the plaza was crowded with people, packed shoulder to shoulder.

Keeping one hand on the open knife in my pocket, I ran toward the little brown man, running on the heads and shoulders of the people in the plaza. The heads and shoulders were of unequal heights and not evenly spaced. I slipped and floundered over them.

The little brown man stood on the steps and laughed until I had almost reached him. Then he ran into the tall building. I chased him up miles of spiral stairway, always just an inch more than a hand's reach behind him. We came to the roof. He ran straight across to the edge and jumped just as one of my hands touched him. His shoulder slid out of my fingers. My hand knocked his sombrero off, and closed on his head. It was a smooth hard round head no larger than a large egg. My fingers went all the way around it. Squeezing his head in one hand, I tried to bring the knife out of my pocket with the other—and realized that I had gone off the edge of the roof with him. We dropped giddily down towards the millions of upturned faces in the plaza, miles down. (pp. 107–8)

Both dreams concern pursuits. One ends well; the other badly. One happens in a lot of places; the other in only one. Both end in the capture of the thing pursued.

The "woman who wore a veil" of the first dream is featureless. The Op does not know what to say to her; she is elusive, disappearing in an emergency, but the Op seeks her faithfully because she is "someone important" to him. Yet though he looks for her everywhere, his efforts do not bring him any closer to her. Still, at length, perhaps because of his long constancy, she finds him. The unparticularized lady with the veil is an idea, perhaps even blindfolded Justice herself; as long as she means something to the Op he seeks her, never really finding her, but the pursuit of her makes it possible for him to receive her. As the Continental Op, working a job that takes him to the same cities Hammett frequented in the course of his Pinkerton duties, the fat man manages to achieve something worth the search, though that something is not manifest in the towns he travels.

The "small brown man who wore an immense sombrero" of the second dream is by contrast more tangible. The Op hates him. It is personal; he is mocked. The Op seeks the little man in a single city in order to use his knife on him. To use the knife he must run on "the heads and shoulders of the people." When he catches up with his quarry, both of them are destroyed. The little man, garbed like a bandit, is the outlaw the Op seeks for visceral reasons rather than the intellectualized idea he subscribes to in his work. The landscape is more confined here, like Poisonville's, in keeping with the particularization of the Op's intention. He must disregard propriety to catch his enemy, even to running roughshod over the citizens of the place. But in the act of taking the law into his own hands to murder his enemy, the Op also murders himself—a mirror of what is happening to him in the story. For in the final analysis the Op is engaged in the willful destruction of his own sensibilities. On the way down he and his adversary are one.

When he wakes he discovers what he had taken to be the small brown man's head grasped in his hand is actually the round handle of an ice pick buried in the prostitute's breast. Such is the Op's loss of belief in himself that he is not sure until the end of the book that he is not in fact her murderer. When Dick Foley presses him on the point, the Op dismisses him, and Foley, white faced, takes his leave deliberately. George J. Thompson III argues that Foley's departure is an act of "faithlessness" which reflects "greater weakness than strength" and "contrasts to the Op's decision to stay and do what he can." [30] On the contrary, Foley's desertion is evidence of Foley's inability to continue conscionably with the Op's kind of case. Foley, "the little Canadian" who "talks like a thrifty man's telegram" [31] and who "could have shadowed a drop of salt water from Golden Gate to Hongkong without ever losing sight of it," [32] is veteran of many earlier Op stories. Notably, he was the Continental man who dove into Oakland Bay in "$106,000 Blood Money" to save Angel Grace Cardigan, and he performs professionally throughout *Red Harvest*. The Op at the outset calls him and Mickey Linehan both "good operatives" (p. 77). Weakness is not in Foley's character as Hammett has drawn him, but prudence is.

After twenty-five murders and various assaults by bludgeon, grenade, and tommy gun, the Op catches a train for Ogden to "fix up" his reports. We are left with an impression of irony, not one of remorse; the reports "didn't fool the Old Man," who gave the Op "merry hell" (p. 142). After terminating his colleague at the end of "$106,000 Blood Money," the Op had at least admitted to weariness that implied some regret; and his voice was "harsh" when he talked about what he had done. Here there is nothing left of Continental's man but his function, like any useful but dangerous piece of equipment.

Hammett's *Red Harvest* owes much to Allan Pinkerton's *The Model Town and the Detectives* (1876). Pinkerton's book dealt with Mariola, a town not far from Chicago having troubles not unlike the problems of Personville: "It was the prevalent opinion in Mariola that a 'gang' or society of desperate criminals existed in and about the city, who were sworn to act in concert and to create a reign of terror in the city" (p. 14).[33] Like the Op, Pinkerton takes up the town-taming job only under a promise of absolute autonomy. ". . . I would undertake to clear the town of its active scoundrels, on condition that I should be allowed to work in my own way without interference by anyone, and that my instructions be obeyed implicitly" (p. 19). Like the Op, too, Pinkerton gets the job done with the help of other operatives. But there are important and suggestive differences between the two books. Pinkerton finds it possible to argue that "criminals, as a rule, are selfish, cowardly, and revengeful: no great number of them could ever remain members of . . . [an organized] society for any length of time" (p. 18). Hammett's story makes clear that criminals may lack nobility, but their organization is endemic to America; old Elihu Willsson heads not a mere aggregation of sneak thieves, but the flow chart of government itself:

> He was president and majority stockholder of the Personville Mining Corporation, ditto of the First National Bank, owner of the *Morning Herald* and the *Evening Herald,* the city's only newspapers, and at least part owner of nearly every other enterprise of any importance. Along with these pieces of property he owned a United States senator, a couple of representatives, the governor, the mayor, and most of the state legislature. (p. 7)

Under the shelter of such institutional sanction, crime is not as easily dismissed as Pinkerton would have it; indeed, the system fosters corruption rather than roots it out. At the end of *Model Town,* Pinkerton can state with satisfaction that "having effectually broken up all the parties of thieves, counterfeiters, burglars, and incendiaries, I left the place to enjoy a career of peace and prosperity" (pp. vii–viii). The Continental Op, however, can offer no such assurances for Personville; he hands it over "all nice and clean and ready to go to the dogs again" (p. 134). The difference between the two books is the inverted progress of fifty years of civic entropy.

Hammett's most famous and most misunderstood novel is *The Maltese Falcon* (1930), featuring the detective who found his blue-jawed incarnation in Humphrey Bogart—Sam Spade. John Paterson, in "A Cosmic View of the Private Eye," sees Hammett's creation as the deification of twentieth-century toughness:

> He is, in the final analysis, the apotheosis of the everyman of good will who, uncertain of his own values and certainly alienated by the values of his time, seeks desperately and mournfully to live without shame, to live without compromise to his integrity. He is everyman's romantic conception of himself: the glorification of toughness, irreverence, and a sense of decency too confused and almost half ashamed to show itself.[34]

George J. Thompson III, in his dissertation on moral vision in Hammett's novels, argues that Hammett "shows through Spade's actions and reactions that ethical action is possible in a world of treachery and deceit, despite personal involvement."[35] He sees Spade's progress in the novel as a "noble adherence to his code."[36] Neither of these views, though traditional support belongs to them, is really an expression of what Hammett was demonstrating in *The Maltese Falcon*. When Spade is compared to "a blond satan" in the first paragraph, Hammett is deliberately setting him forth as a character who is a long way from being a hero. The story is one of losses, among which the greatest are Spade's own, and what is significant about Spade's code is not that he follows it but that it is insufficient.

Spade, who sleeps with his partner's wife but won't marry her, who doesn't cash many checks for strangers, and who hates to be hit without hitting back, is, as he admits, "no Christ" (p. 319).[37] He becomes involved in a quest for a priceless figure of a black bird exacted in payment from the Knights of Rhodes by Emperor Charles V in the twelfth century. The "dingus" turns out to be without value; and it is this fact that is at the center of Hammett's meaning. As Kenneth Millar suggests, "the worthless falcon may symbolize a lost tradition, the great cultures of the Mediterranean past which have become inaccessible to Spade and his generation. Perhaps the bird stands for the Holy Ghost itself, or its absence." [38] But whatever the falcon represents, Spade and the others have been in pursuit of a counterfeit, and in that pursuit they have shown themselves to be similarly counterfeit. Brigid O'Shaughnessy, the black "Leblanc," is a counterfeit innocent; Gutman is a counterfeit sage; Cairo is a counterfeit cosmopolite; and Wilmer, that bleak-eyed beardless boy, is a counterfeit tough guy. Each appears to be what he is not. Worst of all is Spade, a counterfeit hero. The Maltese falcon is the statuary shell of a hunting bird robbed even of its ornamental function; as predatory and as worthless is Spade, the golden boy made of emotional lead.

Much has been written about Spade's awareness of the randomness of reality, his knowledge of "falling beams." He tells the story of a Tacoma real estate agent named Flitcraft who went to lunch one day and didn't come back. Flitcraft had been narrowly missed by a falling steel beam, and the narrowness of his escape showed him that "he, the good-citizen husband-father, could be wiped out between office and restaurant by the accident of a falling beam. He knew then that men died at haphazard like that, and lived only while blind chance spared them" (p. 336). So if life could be ended for him at random, "he would change his life at random by simply going away." Eventually he marries again in Spokane to a woman like his first wife and establishes himself in a life style that resembles the one he left. "He adjusted himself to beams falling," explains Spade, "and then no more of them fell, and he adjusted himself to them not falling" (p. 336). Robert I. Edenbaum writes that "that commonplace enough naturalistic conception of the randomness of the universe is Spade's vision throughout." [39] This may pass for some perception of inner truth on Spade's part, but the point is that Spade, like Flitcraft, is incapable of the kind of emotional involvement that would make such adjustments difficult. Flitcraft can adjust to circumstances easily because he is utterly uncommitted. So can Spade, for the same reason. Flitcraft deserts his family; Spade sleeps with Brigid, then steals from the bed to search her clothes and apartment.

When Effie accuses him of playing around, Spade admits: "I never know what to do or say to women except that way" (p. 311). He searches for his partner's killer not out of grief but because "you're supposed to do something about it" (p. 438). He feels only perfunctorily, and so his act of handing Brigid over to the authorities lacks the stature of great sacrifice. Like Flitcraft, he is going through the motions of what, his awareness of randomness demands; like Flitcraft, he ironically winds up in spite of his efforts exactly as he began—with Iva, whom he does not like.

Spade's defeat of O'Shaughnessy is not the triumph of a morally superior man over a sentimental villainess—it is the empty gesture of an empty man whose occupation is the only thing of value for him—an item, like the falcon, that Hammett shows to be devoid of either warmth or pity. When Effie turns away from Spade at the end of the novel, it is not the "rightness" of what he has done to Brigid that repels her, but his cold-bloodedness in doing it. Spade at the end is "even" with everybody, but there is small satisfaction in it for him. His loss on the final page of Effie Perine is Spade's last and greatest loss, for his secretary is the only character in the book he has been able to respond to at all, and her rejection clearly moves him in a way nothing else in the novel has: "Spade's face became as pale as his collar" (p. 440).

Irving Malin has shown how Spade resorts to the certainty of ceremony—the ritualized rolling of cigarettes, the measured shaking of hands.[40] It is the refuge of a man who, as close friend Lillian Hellman said of Hammett himself, "made up his mind that there was no certainty in any form anywhere."[41] Spade's adherence to the ceremonial extends to his adoption of a behavioral code that is really inverted chivalry: never perform out of sentiment, be a sucker for nobody ("I won't play the sap for you" [p. 437]). Hammett's book is not a novel in praise of that code; it is an examination of its consequences for a man who has nothing else.

Hammett lapsed into literary silence after his last novel, *The Thin Man* (1934), producing all of his fifty-nine short stories and five novels in the twelve years before that. He was thirty-nine. He later contributed film scripts, radio plays, and even a comic strip (*Secret Agent X-9*) about a trimmed-down version of his anonymous Op. Although he had moved to Nob Hill and later Martha's

Vineyard, Hammett's improved financial situation did not prosper his work. He carried on a long and warm relationship with playwright Lillian Hellman, whose writing career began where his ended; *The Children's Hour* (1934) is dedicated to Hammett.

Raymond Chandler, in his celebrated essay "The Simple Art of Murder" (1944), said of Hammett's work that "it was made up of real things"; he praised Hammett as a realist who "took murder out of the Venetian vase and dropped it into the alley" (p. 16).[42] Impatient with the artificiality of the aesthetic school, Chandler characterized the classic English detective story as

> the same grouping of suspects, the same utterly incomprehensible trick of how somebody stabbed Mrs. Pottington Postlethwaite III with the solid platinum poniard just as she flatted on the top note of the "Bell Song" from Lakmé in the presence of fifteen ill-assorted guests; the same ingénue in fur-trimmed pajamas screaming in the night to make the company pop in and out of doors and ball up the timetable; the same moody silence next day as they sit around sipping Singapore slings and sneering at each other, while the flatfeet crawl to and fro under the Persian rugs, with their derby hats on. (pp. 11–12)

By contrast, Dashiell Hammett "wrote scenes that seemed never to have been written before" (p. 17). Chandler's admiration led him to take up Hammett's hard-boiled standard himself, but with important changes.

Chandler was a man of various occupations. He had worked on an apricot ranch, done free-lance journalism, even, for a time, labored as a stringer of tennis rackets. He served with Canada's Gordon Highlanders in World War I and subsequently became an oil executive. But in 1933, at the age of forty-five, he forsook everything else in an effort to become a writer. Chandler published his first story, "Blackmailers Don't Shoot," in *Black Mask* that year. In the pulp stories that followed he evolved the character that was to become Philip Marlowe in his novels, a thinking man's warrior at once saintly and dangerous, raging and mild. "He is the hero, he is everything," wrote Chandler, "he must be a complete man and a common man and yet an unusual man. He must be, to use a rather weathered phrase, a man of honor . . ." (p. 20).

What had been lacking in Hammett's stories for Chandler was the "quality of redemption"; Chandler provided it in Marlowe, who, according to William Patrick Kenney, "establishes in Chandler's novels an explicit moral purpose lacking in Hammett's." [43] Sam Spade and the Continental Op had been sapped, shot at, and slapped around in the name of professionalism; Marlowe does it for an ideal. "He is," Ralph Partridge has written, "the perpetually crucified redeemer of all our modern sins." [44] Marlowe insists on his integrity. Integrity got him into the business; working for the district attorney's office as an investigator, he was fired for "insubordination"—a blanket term for working too hard on matters a more politic man would have met with less zeal. Now a self-employed private eye, Marlowe brings sensitivity and fastidiousness to a profession unaccustomed to either: he will not take loose money, he will not front for a frame, he will not do divorce work. Although he is a "common" man, he sports the accessories of a privileged one—he has been to college, favors a pipe, knows about the diaries of Pepys and the music of Mozart, works out chess problems in his off hours. But he misses the single item style cannot compensate for in America—money. And he is picky about how he earns it. So his manners and mind alienate him from the poor, while his poverty alienates him from the rich, leaving Marlowe to view both with the strong skepticism of the outsider.

Chandler also admired Henry James, and the 1939 prospectus for a novel he never wrote is revealing. He planned "a short, swift, tense, gorgeously written story verging on melodrama. . . . The surface theme is the American in England, the dramatic theme is the decay of the refined character and its contrast with the ingenuous, honest, utterly fearless and generous American of the best type." [45] This Jamesian perspective was essentially the informing vision for all of Chandler's novels, which record the tension between Marlowe and the metropolis. The only difference is the landscape; instead of being English, it is urban American, but the interloper remains the same. Marlowe is perhaps not "ingenuous"; Alistair Cooke's adjective "unfooled" is closer. [46]

But he is separated from his surroundings in the same way Christopher Newman was—or, for that matter, as Raymond Chandler was, bringing his English education to bear on Hollywood film scripts. Notes Philip Durham, "he [Marlowe] remained to the end an idealist and moralist." [47] What this gets Marlowe is not much, except a stoic's stubborn self-reliance. In *Farewell, My Lovely* (1940), Marlowe reflects: "I needed a drink, I needed a lot of life insurance, I needed a vacation, I needed a home in the country. What I had was a coat, a hat and a gun. I put them on and went out of the room" (p. 202).[48] Elsewhere in the novel, Marlowe observes "a shiny black bug with pink spots on" who has somehow contrived to get himself upended in a corner of the homicide squadroom eighteen floors from the street. Marlowe folds the bug in his handkerchief and restores him to the bushes outside. Robert Brown Parker observes that the incident is instructive; "Marlowe cares about the little pink bugs with the feeble legs that get trapped in homicide bureaus and don't know how to get out." [49] Durham suggests the bug "was used to indicate man's struggles and frustrations, man's feebleness in a social order backed by power." [50] But the bug is also illustrative of Marlowe's existential stoicism. Says Marlowe later: "I wondered, in the taxi going home, how long it would take him to make the Homicide Bureau again" (p. 184). It is the detective's recognition that his intervention makes little difference—but he intervenes anyway. This is the "unusual" man Chandler employs "in revolt against a corrupt society." [51]

The corrupt society in which Marlowe moves has been called by W. H. Auden "The Great Wrong Place," a "criminal milieu." [52] But that milieu extends for Marlowe, and for Chandler, far beyond the boundaries of the underworld to the limits of America. Chandler's vision of America was one of lost possibilities. "Philip Marlowe doesn't give a damn who is President," Chandler once replied to a question about his character's voting habits; "neither do I, because I know he will be a politician." [53] Gangs and city councils are indistinguishable in Marlowe's world, where thirty grand buys a mayor and the police chief sits on his hands when he is told to. The cops are corrupt, and even the occasionally honest one is defensive: "We break rules. We have to" (p. 169). In *Farewell, My Lovely,* Marlowe elicits grudging response from hard-nosed Lieutenant Randall of Los Angeles Homicide:

> "Well, if it's a gang job and you break it, that will be the first gang murder solved since I lived in the town. And I could name and describe at least a dozen."
>
> "It's nice of you to say that, Marlowe."
>
> "Correct me if I'm wrong."
>
> "Damn it," he said irritably. "You're not wrong." (p. 165)

One cop Marlowe calls "Hemingway" because of his tendency to repeat himself extends the parameters of graft past those of police administration. The essential problem is a national one:

> "A guy can't stay honest if he wants to," Hemingway said. "That's what's the matter with this country. He gets chiseled out of his pants if he does. You got to play the game dirty or you don't eat. A lot of bastards think all we need is ninety thousand FBI men in clean collars and brief cases. Nuts. The percentage would get them just the way it does the rest of us. You know what I think? I think we gotta make this little world all over again. Now take Moral Rearmament. There you've got something. M.R.A. There you've got something, baby." (p. 196)

Marlowe is an agent of "M.R.A.," but it is Chandler's point that Marlowe is an American failure because of it—he has no money. Marlowe's social station is a consequence of his purity. So is his bitterness. George P. Elliot has observed that "the obvious accomplishment of his [Chandler's] thrillers is to generate a sort of nervous tension which is the literary analogue to the tension generated by just being an American citizen." [54] The consequences of encroaching corruption are illustrated by half-bagged old Jesse Florian, who lives alone with her empties and a radio in a neighborhood that had once been nice: "Folks aren't safe a minute in this town. When I come here twenty-two years ago we didn't lock our doors hardly. Now it's gangsters and crooked police and politicians fightin' each other with machine guns . . ." (p. 92). This kind of uncontested collapse leaves Marlowe a lone gladiator without options. It sours him. There is no way out for Marlowe, nor any expectation at all of lasting change. Increasingly he becomes a man "who needed a drink badly and all the bars were closed" (p. 71).

Chandler expresses all this in a brand of flat relentless poetry. Style was a major concern for Chandler; he had written of Hammett's that "at its worst [it] was as formalized as a page of *Marius the Epicurean;* at its best it could say almost anything. I believe this style, which does not belong to Hammett or to anybody, but is the American language. . . ." [55] Chandler's effort was "to say little and convey much"; [56] he accomplished this with an objective vision that lent profound significance to the surfaces of things. Kenneth Millar notes that Chandler "wrote like a slumming angel"; [57] "Marlowe liberated his author's imagination into an overheard democratic prose that is one of the most effective narrative instruments in recent literature." [58] The cornerstone of Chandler's concrete style is of course the alliterative sardonic simile: "her face fell apart like a bride's pie crust"; [59] "his smile was as faint as a fat lady at a fireman's ball." [60] For Chandler the highly polished eight-cylinder automobile is not a limousine but "the kind of a car you wear your rope pearls in." [61]

"Life as this Irish-American wanted to see it," notes Philip Durham in his book on Chandler, "was not easily expressed in the modern age, for chivalry—once able to stand up to violence—was dead. For Chandler the alternative was to write in a genre in which love had no place." [62] Durham goes on to state that "Chandler was actually writing romantic fiction . . . by simulating reality through a hard-boiled attitude." [63] Not precisely. Chandler's first novel, *The Big Sleep* (1939), is an antiromance; although the book is a careful reworking of portions of four previously published pulp stories ("Finger Man," 1934; "Killer in the Rain," 1935; "The Curtain," 1936; and "Mandarin's Jade," 1937), it is unified by an internal pattern of antiromantic elements.

Set in a sunless Los Angeles, Chandler's story unfolds under a constant cold rain inside "the dark, dripping city" (p. 168).[64] Marlowe observes on page one "a knight in dark armor rescuing a lady" over the entrance doors of the Sternwood mansion. Nubile castle denizen Carmen Sternwood, initially a victim, turns out to resemble more dragon than damsel. Marlowe notes her "little sharp

predatory teeth" and a thumb she nibbles that is "thin and nar-
row like an extra finger, with no curve in the first joint" (p. 3).
The latter detail emphasizes Carmen's nymphomaniacal unnatural-
ness; even her father calls her "a child who likes to pull the wings
off flies" (p. 10). By the end of the novel Carmen's transformation
is complete: as she turns on Marlowe with a gun she emits a
serpentine "hissing sound" which "grew louder, and her face had
the scraped bone look. Aged, deteriorated, [she had] become animal, and not a nice animal" (p. 205). Sir Philip does not save the
lady, one "Silver-Wig" hidden out in a roadhouse; rather she
saves him, loosing his bonds in the manner of the knight's minis-
trations to the blonde over the Sternwood entry. Marlowe goes
after gunman Canino, but dispatches him sans flourish, coming
up from behind.

> He whirled at me. Perhaps it would have been nice to allow
> him another shot or two, just like a gentleman of the old
> school. But his gun was still up and I couldn't wait any
> longer. Not long enough to be a gentleman of the old school.
> I shot him four times. . . . (p. 189)

As Marlowe observes over his chessboard, "Knights had no meaning in this game. It wasn't a game for knights" (p. 146) . Even Marlowe's quest turns out to have been an empty one; Rusty Regan,
the ex-moonshiner he seeks, has been dead for five months by the
time the detective is hired to find him. Near the end of the novel
Marlowe is led to reflect with regret: "Me, I was part of the nasti-
ness now" (p. 216). Nobody lives happily ever after, especially
Marlowe, whose lady, somebody else's wife in the best chivalric
tradition, is missing and stays that way.

> On the way downtown I stopped at a bar and had a couple
> of double Scotches. They didn't do me any good. All they did
> was make me think of Silver-Wig, and I never saw her again.
> (p. 216)

Marlowe is left to the only company he can count on, the whiskey
he uses "to keep warm and interested" (p. 27).

Julian Symons has recognized that Chandler had originally

meant to call Marlowe "Mallory," linking his character to the
recorder of chivalric dissolution in *Morte d'Arthur*,[65] but the
final appellation is also significant. If "Philip," a doff of the hat
to the incomparable Sidney, retains some sense of the chivalric,
"Marlowe" incorporates the more sinister flavor of magnificent
excess in an earlier Marlowe's renderings of Renaissance over-
reachers—and a dash of the detachment of another observing outsider, Conrad's Marlowe.

Marlowe's disaffection is clear in *The Big Sleep* ("The hell with
the rich. They made me sick" [p. 59]), a disaffection that worsens
later. *The Lady in the Lake* (1943) is Marlowe's *Paradise Lost*,
recording his vision of irrevocable Edenic loss. Robert Brown
Parker has written that "with the big woods gone, and the prairie
beribboned with highway, the only alternatives are to work within
the establishment, and either adopt its values, or oppose it with
one's private moral judgment." [66] The loss of the "big woods" in
Lady confirms Marlowe's choice as the latter one, but his choice
solves little.

Marlowe drives outside the city to a region that proves the limits
of corruption are not urban. The war, that larger conflict beyond
the story, has touched Puma Lake:

> The Puma Lake dam had an armed sentry at each end and
> one in the middle. The first one I came to had me close all
> the windows of the car before crossing the dam. About a
> hundred yards away from the dam a rope with cork floats
> barred the pleasure boats from coming any closer. Beyond
> these details the war did not seem to have done anything to
> Puma Lake. (p. 26) [67]

Other things had. The first man Marlowe meets there is a de-
formed caretaker with an ax in his hand. Marlowe is sensitive to
the flora and fauna of the region—no one has a sharper botanical
eye—but things are happening to Little Faun Lake and environs
that have nothing to do with nature. A movie company has
installed a millwheel, for example, and somebody else has installed
a corpse. The body turns out to be the person Marlowe was hired
to find, as in *The Big Sleep;* the other members of the resort area

are in scarcely better condition, as Marlowe's description of them at an inn reveals:

> The whole place was filled to overflowing with males in leisure jackets and liquor breaths and females in high-pitched laughs, oxblood fingernails and dirty knuckles. The manager of the joint, a low budget tough guy in shirt sleeves and a mangled cigar, was prowling around the room with watchful eyes. At the cash desk a pale-haired man was fighting to get the war news on a small radio that was as full of static as the mashed potatoes were full of water. In the deep back corner of the room, a hillbilly orchestra of five pieces, dressed in ill-fitting white jackets and purple shirts, was trying to make itself heard above the brawl at the bar and smiling glassily into the fog of cigarette smoke and the blur of alcoholic voices. At Puma Point summer, that lovely season, was in full swing. (p. 51)

Marlowe, in contrast to his associations, carries on soberly and with a sense of sacrifice. That does not change his world, but it makes living in it possible for him.

He is not like the cops. Bay City sleuth Captain Webber, in an uncharacteristically reflective moment, shares his perceptions on police work with Marlowe: "Police business . . . is a hell of a problem. It's a good deal like politics. It asks for the highest type of men, and there's nothing in it to attract the highest men. So we have to work with what we get . . ." (p. 150). Marlowe, who *is* one of the best men, has to see himself in consequence as quixotic, perhaps a little ridiculous. His self-mockery supports the detective's increasing embarrassment at the knightly role. "I put my plain card, the one without the tommy gun in the corner, on the desk," he notes wryly (p. 2). Later he engages in this exchange:

> "And what did you say your name was?"
> "Vance," I said. "Philo Vance."
> "And what company are you employed with, Mr. Vance?"
> "I'm out of work right now," I said. "Until the police commissioner gets into a jam again." (p. 89)

Marlowe and Vance are worlds apart, but Marlowe finds himself
at times sharing Vance's role as social anachronism. What separates
them is Marlowe's unrelenting awareness of evil: he has seen the
sewers. They are not distant, and he does not have to travel as far
as Puma Point to find them. All he need do is engage his eyes. In
jail Marlowe finds himself thinking about it:

> I sat down on the bunk again. It was made of flat steel slats
> with a thin mattress over them. Two dark gray blankets were
> folded on it quite neatly. It was a very nice jail. It was on the
> twelfth floor of the new city hall. It was a very nice city hall.
> Bay City was a very nice place. People lived there and thought
> so. If I lived there, I would probably think so. I would see the
> nice blue bay and the cliffs and the yacht harbor and the quiet
> streets of houses, old houses brooding under old trees and new
> houses with sharp green lawns and wire fences and staked
> saplings set into the parkway in front of them. I knew a girl
> who lived at Twenty-fifth Street. It was a nice street. She was
> a nice girl. She liked Bay City.
> She wouldn't think about the Mexican and Negro slums
> stretched out on the dismal flats south of the old interurban
> tracks. Nor of the waterfront dives along the flat shore south
> of the cliffs, the sweaty little dance halls on the pike, the mari-
> huana joints, the narrow fox faces watching over the tops of
> newspapers in far too quiet hotel lobbies, nor the pickpockets
> and grifters and con men and drunk rollers and pimps and
> queens on the board walk. (p. 143)

Marlowe thinks of them—perhaps too much. By the end of *Lady*
one of the sentries on the dam shoots the murderer Degarmo (a
rogue cop), and another body is fished from the lake. But the depth
of Marlowe's disaffection is not yet.

That comes in *The Little Sister* (1949), Chandler's strongest—
and angriest—book. In it Hollywood becomes a metaphor for mis-
placed American values. Chandler had a paradigm love-hate relationship with Hollywood; he was responsible for three fine film
scripts (*Double Indemnity*, 1944, with Billy Wilder; *The Blue
Dahlia*, 1946; and *Strangers on a Train*, 1951, with Czenzi Or-
monde), but his Quaker's moral sense was offended by what he

termed "the Hollywood manner, which is a chronic case of spurious excitement over absolutely nothing." [68] Chandler saw Hollywood as an American microcosm. When he wrote "Oscar Night in Hollywood" (1948), he complained of the artificial polling system for Academy Awards, which for Chandler were "ballyhooed, pushed, yelled, screamed, and in every way propagandized into the voters so incessantly, in the weeks before the final balloting, that everything except the golden aura of the box office is forgotten." [69] . . . "We elect Congressmen and Presidents in much the same way," observed Chandler grimly. In *The Little Sister,* Hollywood is the skull beneath the southern California skin: "Real cities have . . . some individual bony structure under the muck. Los Angeles has Hollywood—and hates it" (p. 203).[70]

Marlowe encounters in the course of the case a producer named Oppenheimer who wanders aimlessly about his studio with three boxers and whose chief recreation is watching his charges pee—on the flowers, the carpet, his desk, everywhere. Oppenheimer descants on the movie industry to a fascinated Marlowe. "The motion picture business," explains the mogul, "is the only business in the world in which you can make all the mistakes there are and still make money." Art has nothing to do with it: "Doesn't matter a damn what they do or how they do it. Just give me fifteen hundred theatres" (p. 137). Marlowe, who earns every dime of his forty dollars a day and expenses (up from a preinflationary twenty-five), is the only authentic workman around; the tendency is rather toward overcommitment than fraud: "In my business a fellow does what he can to protect a client. Sometimes he goes too far" (p. 187). In the Hollywood moral vacuum, Marlowe's outrage takes him farther than he has ever gone. But he alone remains unfooled. When someone suggests he is falling in love with movie bombshell Mavis Weld, Marlowe's response is measured:

"That would be kind of silly. I could sit in the dark with her and hold hands, but for how long? In a little while she will drift off into a haze of glamour and expensive clothes and froth and unreality and muted sex. She won't be a real person any more. Just a voice from a sound track, a face on a screen. I'd want more than that." (p. 278)

The detective cannot be led astray by love, but he can by responsibility; it is morals, not women, that draw Marlowe to the brink.

"I was far outside the law already," he reflects after a long chain of breakings and enterings and assorted suppressions of evidence (p. 173). He has never been closer to the behavior of the police he abhors, but Marlowe can justify his machinations in the name of protecting a client. The rogue cop is something Marlowe understands very well; he shows how well in the face of a threatened third degree:

> [Lieutenant] Maglashan took a heavy worn pigskin glove out of his pocket and put it on his right hand and flexed his fingers.
>
> "What's that for?" Biefus asked him.
>
> "I bite my nails at times," Maglashan said. "Funny. Only bite 'em on my right hand." He raised his slow eyes to stare at me. "Some guys are more voluntary than others," he said idly. "Something to do with the kidneys, they tell me. I've known guys of the not so voluntary type that had to go to the can every fifteen minutes for weeks after they got voluntary. Couldn't seem to hold water."
>
> "Just think of that," Biefus said wonderingly.
>
> "Then there's the guys can't talk above a husky whisper," Maglashan went on. "Like punch-drunk fighters that have stopped too many with their necks."
>
> Maglashan looked at me. It seemed to be my turn.
>
> "Then there's the type that won't go to the can at all," I said. "They try too hard. Sit in a chair like this for thirty hours straight. Then they fall down and rupture a spleen or burst a bladder. They overco-operate. And after sunrise court, when the tank is empty, you find them dead in a dark corner. Maybe they ought to have seen a doctor, but you can't figure everything, can you, Lieutenant?" (p. 187)

Marlowe knows the motivations of a Maglashan are more complex than simple sadism; they are the frustrated result of betrayed loyalties and routine brutalities that come from being closed in "the cold half-lit world where always the wrong thing happens and never the right" (p. 89). Such cops

had the calm weathered faces of healthy men in hard condition. They had the eyes they always have, cloudy and gray
like freezing water. The firm set mouth, the hard little
wrinkles at the corners of the eyes, the hard hollow meaning-
less stare, not quite cruel and a thousand miles from kind.
The dull ready-made clothes, worn without style, with a sort
of contempt; the look of men who are poor and yet proud
of their power, watching always for ways to make it felt, to
shove it into you and twist it and grin and watch you squirm,
ruthless without malice, cruel yet not always unkind. What
would you expect them to be? Civilization had no meaning
for them. All they saw of it was the failures, the dirt, the dregs,
the aberrations and the disgust. (p. 196)

Which is all Marlowe sees. *The Little Sister* is the account of a
Marlowe on his way to becoming a Maglashan; the same fierce
pride is there, the same suppressed fury. Marlowe's thoughts on
what is happening to his city show the extent of his anger, tripped
by increasingly insignificant gestures:

I stopped at Fairfax with the green light to let a man make a
left turn. Horns blew violently behind. When I started again
the car that had been right behind swung out and pulled
level and a fat guy in a sweatshirt yelled:
"Aw go get yourself a hammock!"
He went on, cutting in so hard that I had to brake.
"I used to like this town," I said, just to be saying something and not to be thinking too hard. "A long time ago.
There were trees along Wilshire Boulevard. Beverly Hills
was a country town. Westwood was bare hills and lots offering
at eleven hundred dollars and no takers. Hollywood was a
bunch of frame houses on the interurban line. Los Angeles
was just a big dry sunny place with ugly houses and no style,
but good-hearted and peaceful. It had the climate they just
yap about now. People used to sleep out on porches. Little
groups who thought they were intellectual used to call it the
Athens of America. It wasn't that, but it wasn't a neon-lighted
slum either. . . .
"Now we get characters like this [mobster] Steelgrave own-

ing restaurants. We get guys like that fat boy who bawled me
out back there. We've got the big money, the sharp shooters,
the percentage workers, the fast-dollar boys, the hoodlums out
of New York and Chicago and Detroit—and Cleveland. We've
got the flash restaurants and night clubs they run and the
hotels and apartment houses they own, and the grifters and
con men and female bandits that live in them. The luxury
trades, the pansy decorators, the Lesbian dress designers, the
riffraff of a big hard-boiled city with no more personality
than a paper cup. Out in the fancy suburbs dear old Dad is
reading the sports page in front of a picture window, with his
shoes off, thinking he is high class because he has a three-car
garage. Mom is in front of her princess dresser trying to paint
the suitcases out from under her eyes. And Junior is clamped
onto the telephone calling up a succession of high-school girls
that talk pigeon English and carry contraceptives in their
make-up kit." (pp. 202–3)

Marlowe becomes more and more shrill as he nears the end of
the novel. Involved in a family in which two members engage in
a plot to blackmail the third and one thousand dollars is bribe
enough to pay a sister to finger her brother, the eye's continuing
revision of evidence is performed to preserve the one person in
whom he sees value, but the rareness of that value is not sustaining
to self-mocking, progress-bemoaning Marlowe.

> The Luger under my arm and the .32 in my hand made me
> tough. Two-gun Marlowe, the kid from Cyanide Gulch. (p.
> 214)

It is not long before he is talking from the side of his mouth all
the time. Standing at the site of a stage-managed murder, Marlowe waits for the law: "No siren. But the sound of a car coming
up the hill at last. I went out to meet it, me and my beautiful
dream" (p. 231). Like Gatsby, he can see the lights of a big house
("Some Hollywood big shot, probably . . ."), but there is not
even a Daisy at the end of a dock for Marlowe. His dream is a
nightmare.

It comes as little surprise that Marlowe, that mean-eyed moralist, ultimately cracks. Dolores Gonzales, murderess and movie star, remains by the end of the book above retribution: "nothing would ever touch her, not even the law" (p. 277). As Marlowe leaves her he takes away an image of a woman "reeking with sex. Utterly beyond the moral laws of this or any world I could imagine" (p. 278). So he allows her to be killed. He passes her irate husband in the hall, and Marlowe knows he has his wife's murder on his mind. "Perhaps," the detective muses after the husband has killed his wife and himself, "I ought to have stopped him. Perhaps I had a hunch what he would do, and deliberately let him do it" (p. 280). Perhaps. Marlowe does not allow himself to dwell on the thought; but his method smacks of the engineered suicides arranged by his scorned predecessor, Philo Vance.

If, as Philip Durham argues, "Chandler's hero is the all-American boy with whom the reader easily identifies himself, the rough man of action who would never harm a fly but would stamp out injustice with a vigorous passion," [71] there is at least room for pause about Marlowe's lack of self-knowledge in his sort of crusade. Herbert Ruhm's statement that Marlowe "believes in truth, and justice, and honesty and fidelity, and he will go to any length to protect those in whom he sees these qualities" is two-edged: [72] in the absence of law, "any length" involves some distance. Marlowe is not amoral, like Sam Spade or the Continental Op; he is an advocate whose morality motivates him. He works not for the job but for the client. "Sometimes he goes too far."

In the ten years that remained of his life Chandler wrote two more Marlowe novels, one good, one less so (*The Long Goodbye*, 1954; and *Playback*, 1958). He died in 1959, one month after having been elected president of the Mystery Writers of America.

"I do not see who can succeed Raymond Chandler," Maugham wrote. [73] He meant that there seemed little left to be done with the private eye novel, but there were noteworthy changes. These were, with few exceptions, degenerative rather than developmental. Chandler popularized the form Hammett created; later writers, less successful than their predecessors in matters of style and character, made overt those qualities of cheerful sadism and puritan rage latent in the received material. The sardonic slang soon became secondhand; the characters too often stepped straight from the stockroom. But looming ever larger as holy arbiter of earthly ills was the private eye hero, now pursuing not merely his profession nor even the protection of his clients but intensely personal visions of divine judgment. He answered now a Call.

The most materially successful of Chandler's heirs is ex-army pilot Mickey (Frank Morrison) Spillane, who believes with Samuel Johnson that nobody but a blockhead writes for anything but money. Spillane started out scripting dialogue for the voice balloons in comic books like *Captain America, Submariner,* and *The Human Torch.* When comic books began to pay less well (at their height it was possible to get twelve dollars a page for grinding out forty or fifty of them a day), he started a novel featuring an action-comics character named Mike Danger who became New York private eye Mike Hammer. The novel was *I, the Jury* (1947), the first of a string of what Spillane would call "adult comic books." He wrote it in a tent while he built his first house, trowel in one hand and instruction book in the other, and it was typical of the man that no notion of difficulty kept him from accomplishing either the first time. Twenty novels and as many years later he had become the largest-selling author in the English —or any other—language, and if the essence of his work was fantasy, Spillane made his dreams participatory by starring in one film (*Ring of Fear,* 1954) as himself and in another (*The Girl Hunters,* 1963) as alter ego Hammer, posing his wife for the first nude hardback dust jacket (*The Erection Set,* 1972) and producing a film of one of his stories for her to star in (*Erection Set* again).[74] Recently Spillane appeared as a murdered popular author suspiciously like himself in an installment of the Peter Falk television series *Columbo.* Living out his reveries in print, Spillane carried the hard-boiled hero to his attenuated extreme—Nemesis as Superman with sexual drive.

I, the Jury begins with Hammer's entry into the official investigation of his best friend's murder. Hammer is demonstrably upset at the passing of "Jack, the guy who said he'd give his right arm for a friend and did it when he stopped a bastard of a Jap from slitting me in two" (p. 5).[75] Hammer announces at once: "I'm going to get the one that did this" (p. 6). Pat Chambers, a police captain and friend of Mike's, protests. This is the occasion for Hammer to express his sentiments on legal procedure:

"Okay, Pat. . . . You have a job to do, but so have I. Jack was about the best friend I ever had. We lived together and fought together. And by Christ, I'm not letting the killer go through the tedious process of the law. You know what happens, damn it. They get the best lawyer there is and screw up the whole thing and wind up a hero. . . . No, damn it. A jury is cold and impartial like they're supposed to be, while some snotty killer makes them pour tears as he tells how his client was insane at the moment or had to shoot in self-defense. Swell. The law is fine. But this time I'm the law. . . ." (p. 7)

Later, when Chambers argues that the cops are not exactly dumb and can find a few answers of their own, Hammer concedes they can think as fast as he can, but they "haven't got the ways and means of doing the dirty work." Complains Hammer: "Cops can't break a guy's arm to make him talk, and they can't shove his teeth in with the muzzle of a .45 to remind him that [they] aren't fooling" (p. 11). Legal punctilio is not Hammer's strong suit; "Instead of fooling around," Hammer yawns "I brought out the skeleton keys" (p. 40).

It is Hammer's role to be a sort of democratic scourge, a cleanser of community sinks. This is a role that demands at once Hammer's contempt for the common man's inability to adjust an evil world and his approval of that man's values. "People," ruminates Hammer. "How incredibly stupid they could be sometimes. . . . But in the end the people have their justice. They get it through guys like me . . ." (p. 16). Fulfilling that role brings Hammer to the heights of middle-American prejudice. His adversaries are significant: in *Jury*'s first fifty pages he works over two blacks and a pair of homosexuals; by the end of the book he has roughed up two more "pansies" and a college dean as well, exacting the kind of revenge upon minorities and intellectuals that only the hostile, threatened cracker requires. Hammer feels a kindred resentment for the rich. When he asks a prostitute who attends the "shows" performed late in city bagnios, she responds: "Just prosperous people." Thinks Mike: "I knew the kind. Fat greasy people from out of town. Slick city boys who played the angles and were willing to shell out the dough. Rich jokers of both sexes who liked smut and filth and didn't care where they got it. A pack of queers who enjoyed exotic, sadistic sex. Nasty people . . ." (p. 81). Nor is self-knowledge Hammer's strong suit; it is he who watches with interest while Charlotte, the murderess who happens also to be a threatening high-brow female psychiatrist, slowly strips off her clothes in front of him (*"she was a real blonde"* [p. 171]) and then shoots her, low in the belly. The scene is a parody of Sam Spade's renunciation of Brigid in *The Maltese Falcon;* once again the girl gets thrown over, only this time she won't be out in twenty years. "Beautiful as you are, as much as I almost loved you, I sentence you to death" (p. 173). And Hammer, who feels "pretty good" after knocking a couple of heads together (p. 142) and maintains he will "enjoy" putting a bullet in the killer (p. 95), can actually justify his labors with the simple declaration: "I hate rats that kill for the fun of it" (p. 107).

One Lonely Night (1951) recounts Mike's campaign against the Commies. The book begins with Hammer's night memory of a trial held over him because he "knocked off somebody who needed knocking off bad" (p. 6).[76] The judge sermonized at him, which rankles, and the detective had been led from court by his sympathetic secretary, Velda: "Let's get out of here, Mike. I hate people with little minds" (p. 7). As Hammer ponders the vagaries of "too slow justice" (p. 9), the implication unfolds that his passion for murder is the psychotic result of wartime experience:

> The crazy music that had been in my head ever since I came back from those dusks and dawns started again, a low steady beat overshadowed by the screaming of brassier, shriller instruments that hadn't been invented yet. They shouted and pounded a symphony of madness and destruction while I held my hands over my ears and cursed until they stopped. (p. 8)

The course of his midnight meditations is broken when a woman runs to him on a deserted bridge. Hammer generously kills her pursuer, but the woman takes one look at the "mask of kill-lust" on his face and jumps over the rail. What chagrin: "I did it again, I killed somebody else!" (p. 11). Hammer spends the remainder of the book seeking out the identities of his victims—and incidentally seeking out his own. He even wonders, in moments of weakness, if the judge had been correct in castigating him:

> *The judge had been right!* There had been too many of those dusks and dawns; there had been pleasure in all that killing, an obscene pleasure that froze your face in a grin even when you were charged with fear. Like when I cut down that Jap with his own machete and laughed like hell while I made slices of his scrawny body, then went on to do the same thing again because it got to be fun. . . . I enjoyed the killing, every bit of it. (p. 144)

But at length Hammer realizes that he has indeed been right all along; nuts to the judge.

> *I lived only to kill the scum and the lice that wanted to kill themselves. I lived to kill so that others could live. . . . I was the evil that opposed other evil, leaving the good and the meek in the middle to live and inherit the earth!* (p. 149)

World without end, amen.

The most horrendous "scum" and "lice" are of course the Communists. Hammer does not like the Communists. Nor does he like people who listen to them. In Union Square he mingles with groups gathered to stump for causes that irritate him. "The sheep" are a "seedy bunch"; notes Mike, "a guy who looked like a girl and a girl who looked like a guy altered their course to join one group." Worse, beefs Hammer,

> I had to stand there and hear just why anybody that fought the war was a simple-minded fool, why anybody who tolerated the foreign policy of this country was a Fascist, why anybody who didn't devote his soul and money to the enlightenment of the masses was a traitor to the people. (p. 26)

Hammer wangles his way into a cell meeting and later admits "I wanted to feel the butt of an M-1 against my shoulder pointing at those bastards up there on the rostrum and feel the pleasant impact as it spit slugs into their guts" (p. 71). At moments he becomes strident with rage:

> "I hate everything they stand for. I'm sorry we have to tolerate it. We ought to do what they would have done a hundred years ago."
>
> "Stop talking nonsense" [advises stolid Pat Chambers]. "You're an American now."
>
> "Sure I am, and I want to stay here. If you want a democracy you have to fight for it. Why not now before it's too late? That's the trouble, we're getting soft. They push us all around the block and we let them get away with it!" (p. 90)

At moments, he roars.

> *Go after the big boys. Oh, don't arrest them, don't treat them to the democratic process of courts and law . . . do the same thing to them that they'd do to you! Treat 'em to the unglorious taste of sudden death. . . . Kill 'em left and right, show 'em that we aren't so soft after all. Kill, kill, kill, kill!* (pp. 91–92)

Nobody thinks in italics like Mike Hammer.

The problem again is distinguishing Mike from his enemies. His brand of righteousness smacks of what he terms the villainy of the enemy. Hammer sizes up the opposition this way:

> They had a slogan that the end justifies the means.
> They would kill to accomplish a purpose.
> They would wreck everything to gain their ends, even if they had to build again on the wreckage. (p. 130)

And here is Hammer:

> . . . some day, maybe, some day I'd stand on the steps of the Kremlin with a gun in my fist and I'd yell for them to come out and if they wouldn't I'd go in and get them and when I had them lined up against the wall I'd start shooting until all I had left was a row of corpses that bled on the cold floors

and in whose thick red blood would be the promise of a peace that would stick for more generations than I'd live to see. (p. 121)

In Hammer there is the same strong moral line, the same we/ they attitude driving him to do murder for what he terms a greater good, that he deplores in "the Commies." The root of it is Bible Belt fundamentalism. The powerful rhythms of Spillane's recorded rage show a stylistic debt to the King James text. Hammer is capable of prayer, and he resorts to an Old Testament vision of himself as God's agent in order to justify the carnage. When Velda becomes initiate to slaughter by blowing one of the devil's minions to kingdom come with her "nasty little .32," this exchange ensues:

[Velda:] "Maybe I should feel ashamed and sinful, but I don't. I'm glad I shot him. I'm glad I had the chance to do it and not you. I wanted to, do you understand that?"

[Mike:] "I understand completely. I know how you feel because it's how I feel. There's no shame or sin in killing a killer. David did it when he knocked off Goliath. Saul did it when he slew his tens of thousands. There's no shame to killing an evil thing. As long as you have to live with the fact you might as well enjoy it." (p. 99)

Spillane said once he is so far right he practically falls off the edge; [77] Mike Hammer leaps headlong.

Hammer achieves a curious identity with the murderer in *One Lonely Night*. Oscar Deamer is the demented twin of politician Lee. Escaping an institution, he changes places with his brother, killing him and taking on the role of reformer. He actually serves as an agent for the Communists. Thus Oscar, who seems to be a public hope, is in reality a private menace. Hammer is also a split personality who calls himself the instrument of justice, but whose evident madness manifests itself in murder that makes him more society's threat than its salvation. Hammer says of Deamer something that might be said of himself: "I've seen evangelists with faces like that, unswerving, devoted to their duty" (p. 63). He and Deamer achieve a terrible union in the final chapter, alone together on the bridge where the story began. After explaining why he will kill him, Hammer proceeds in what is a grim burlesque of the sexual act:

> I turned him around to face me, to let him look at what I was and see how I enjoyed his dying. The man who had thrown a lot of people on the long road to nowhere was a gibbering idiot slobbering at the mouth. I had his neck in my one hand and squeezed and squeezed and squeezed until my fingers were buried in the flesh of his throat and his hands clawed at my arm frantically, trying to tear me away.
>
> I laughed a little bit. It was the only sound in the night. I laughed while his tongue swelled up and bulged out with his eyes and his face turning black. I held him until he was down on his knees and dead as he ever was going to be. . . . (p. 158)

The two killers are joined, the only difference between them the fact that Deamer dies and Hammer does not. Even the names match like two halves of a vaudeville team.

The apogee of Hammer's italic fury occurs when he comes upon the kidnapped Velda, strung from the ceiling and in the hands of guess who:

> *She was stark naked.*
>
> *She hung from the rafters overhead by a rope that chewed into her wrists, while her body twisted slowly in the single light of the electric lantern! The guy in the pork-pie hat waited until she turned to face him then brought the knotted rope around with all the strength of his arm and I heard it bite into her flesh . . . while the rest slobbered with the lust and pleasure of this example of what was yet to come, even drooled with the passion that was death made slow in the fulfillment of the philosophy that lived under a red flag!* (pp. 148–49)

Yet Hammer has been guilty of the same kind of sadism only one chapter earlier. Having decided to punish socialite Ethel for her foolishness in being a part of the Party, Hammer has her disrobe and then takes off his own belt.

A naked woman and a leather belt. I looked at her, so bare and so pretty, hands pressed for support against the paneling, legs spread apart to hold a precarious balance, a flat stomach hollowed under the fear that burned her body a faint pink, lovely smooth breasts, firm with terrible excitement, rising and falling with every gasping breath. A gorgeous woman who had been touched by the hand of the devil.

I raised the belt and swung it and heard the sharp crack of the leather against her thighs and her scream. . . . (p. 117)

Hammer is at his berserk best in battles with the violators of his Velda, and it is difficult to see where his methods differ from their own. The madness in him is indisputable as he brings a tommy gun to bear, the "crazy music" welling up to crescendo inside his incredible snapped head:

They heard my scream and the awful roar of the gun and the slugs tearing into bone and guts and it was the last they heard. They went down as they tried to run and felt their insides tear out and spray against the walls. . . .

I laughed and laughed while I put the second clip in the gun. I knew the music in my head was going wild this time, but I was laughing too hard to enjoy it. I went around the room and kicked them over on their backs and if they had faces left I made sure they didn't. I saved the last burst for the bastard who was MVD in a pork-pie hat and who looked like a kid. A college boy. He was still alive when he stared into the flame that spit out of the muzzle only an inch from his nose. (p. 149)

Something too much of this: Hammer's "wonderful knowledge that you're hot and right" (p. 146) has made an animal of him.

At this writing, *One Lonely Night* has sold more than five million copies.

Hammer is back against the Reds again in *The Girl Hunters* (1962). He has been drunk for seven years and is down now to one-sixty-eight from two-o-five because he sent Velda out on a case from which she has not returned; now a murder has been done that suggests she is alive somewhere, and Hammer snaps out of it to find her. His adversary is "The Dragon," a Russian intelligence team that ends up consisting of a Soviet who looks like an Indian and the wife of a dead senator. An FBI man gives Mike an official capacity and the legal right to carry a gun. In keeping with the times, Hammer's mission has grown to global proportions: "It was a world conquest scheme" (p. 116).[78] Older and less inclined to write at the top of his voice, Spillane still allows Hammer his evangelical mood; as federal agent Art Rickerby observes, "You're a killer, Mike. You've always been a killer. Somehow your actions have been justified and I think righteously so . . ." (p. 150). So trench-coated Mike once again engineers the end of his enemy outside "the new Babylon that was the city" (p. 184); he works the Indian over and leaves him with his hand nailed to the floor of a barn for safekeeping, then plugs the barrels of a shotgun so the senator's wife will blow her head off when she uses it.

Although Spillane disclaims any artistic pretentions ("Creative urge, hell—I get a money urge"),[79] it would be a mistake not to call him a craftsman; he writes with a sense of pace and a break-neck style that even serious critics admit keeps them turning the pages. Like Poe his first interest is his ending, often saving a twist for the very last lines: "The first chapter sells this book—the last sells the next one." And Spillane sells them; if sensationalism is a peddling point, he has as well the something else that keeps him ahead of his imitators. Such an appetite for Spillane material implies that there is a wide audience for vengeance stories offering a hero whose scruples are invisible, though the lack of them may be obscured under an occluding cloud of conservatism. The revealing truth about the cases of Mike Hammer is that he is never hired to carry them out—he operates out of personal interest alone. Thus the professional ethic gives way completely to a private one as the detective's motivating force. Hammer, middle class and anti-intellectual, embodying the middle-class man's suspicion of government and faith in the will of "the people," is easy for an American to identify with; his vendettas are his readers'. Another apostle of popular violence, film actor Clint Eastwood, was once asked about the massacre in his movies, and Eastwood explained the audience for it this way: ". . . it's not the blood-letting or whatever that people come to see in the movies. It's vengeance. Getting even is a very important thing with the public. They go to work every day for some guy who's rude and they can't stand and they have to take it. Then they go see me on the screen and I just kick the shit out of him." [80] So does Spillane. He fulfills the locus for the private eye's arc of engagement: while Hammett's hero did his job and Chandler's served his client, Spillane's mad angel visits damnation on those who cross him. For the public good.

NOTES

1. Ron Goulart, Introduction to *The Hardboiled Dicks: An Anthology and Study of Pulp Detective Fiction* (Los Angeles: Sherbourne Press, 1965), p. xi.

2. Frank Gruber, *The Pulp Jungle* (Los Angeles: Sherbourne Press, 1967), p. 23.

3. Thomas Sturak, "Horace McCoy, Captain Shaw, and the *Black Mask*," in *The Mystery and Detection Annual*, ed. Donald K. Adams (Pasadena, Calif.: Castle Press, 1972), p. 139.

4. Goulart, p. xii.

5. Gruber, p. 101.

6. Quoted in William F. Nolan, *Dashiell Hammett: A Casebook* (Santa Barbara, Calif.: McNally and Loftin, 1969), p. 24.

7. Quoted in Goulart, pp. xi–xii.

8. Quoted in Philip Durham, "The Black Mask School," in *Tough Guy Writers of the Thirties*, ed. David Madden (Carbondale and Edwardsville: Southern Illinois University Press, 1968), p. 58.

9. Quoted in Durham, "Black Mask," p. 56.

10. Quoted in Erle Stanley Gardner, "Getting Away with Murder," *Atlantic*, January 1965, p. 72.

11. .Gardner, p. 73.

12. Gruber, p. 145.

13. Durham, "Black Mask," p. 52.

14. Nolan, p. 40.

15. Durham, "Black Mask," p. 60.

16. Nolan, p. 18.

17. Citations to Hammett's Op stories are from *The Big Knockover: Selected Stories and Short Novels of Dashiell Hammett*, ed. Lillian Hellman (New York: Vintage, 1972), with the noted exceptions.

18. Dashiell Hammett, "The Whosis Kid," in *The Return of the Continental Op* (New York: Dell, 1945), p. 60.

19. Durham, "Black Mask," p. 61.

20. Hammett, "Whosis," p. 41.

21. Hammett, "Whosis," p. 50.

22. Quoted in Nolan, p. 27.

23. Hammett, "Whosis," p. 44.

24. "The Big Knockover" and "$106,000 Blood Money" were later collected and printed as the "novel" *Blood Money* (Cleveland: World, 1943).

25. Durham, "Black Mask," p. 51.

26. Ross Macdonald [Kenneth Millar], "The Writer as Detective Hero," *Show*, January 1965, p. 35.

27. Robert Brown Parker, "The Violent Hero, Wilderness Heritage and Urban Reality: A Study of the Private Eye in the Novels of Dashiell Hammett, Raymond Chandler and Ross Macdonald," Diss., Boston University, 1971, p. 102.

28. George J. Thompson III, "The Problem of Moral Vision in Dashiell Hammett's Detective Novels," Diss., University of Connecticut, 1972, p. 38.

29. Citations to Hammett's *Red Harvest* are from *The Novels of Dashiell Hammett* (New York: Knopf, 1965), pp. 3–142.

30. Thompson, p. 31.

31. Hammett, *Knockover*, p. 204.

32. Hammett, *Knockover*, p. 378.

33. Citations to Pinkerton's *The Model Town and the Detectives* are from the G. W. Carleton edition (New York, 1876).

34. John Paterson, "A Cosmic View of the Private Eye," *Saturday Review*, August 22, 1953, p. 31.

35. Thompson, p. 86.

36. Thompson, p. 94.

37. Citations to Hammett's *The Maltese Falcon* are from *The Novels of Dashiell Hammett* (New York: Knopf, 1965), pp. 293–440.

38. Macdonald, p. 35.

39. Robert I. Edenbaum, "The Poetics of the Private Eye: The Novels of Dashiell Hammett," in *Tough Guy Writers of the Thirties*, ed. David Madden (Carbondale and Edwardsville: Southern Illinois University Press, 1968) , p. 83.

40. Irving Malin, "Focus on 'The Maltese Falcon': The Metaphysical Falcon," in *Tough Guy Writers of the Thirties*, ed. David Madden (Carbondale and Edwardsville: Southern Illinois University Press, 1968), p. 105.

41. Quoted in Nora Ephron, "Lillian Hellman Walking, Cooking, Writing, Talking," *New York Times Book Review*, September 23, 1973, p. 51.

42. Citations to Chandler's "The Simple Art of Murder" are from

The Simple Art of Murder (1950; rpt. New York: Ballantine, 1972), pp. 1–22.

43. William Patrick Kenney, "The Dashiell Hammett Tradition and the Modern Detective Novel," Diss., University of Michigan, 1964, p. 130.

44. Ralph Partridge, "Detection and Thrillers," *New Statesman and Nation,* January 9, 1954, p. 47.

45. Dorothy Gardiner and Katherine Sorley Walker, eds., *Raymond Chandler Speaking* (Freeport, N.Y.: Books for Libraries Press, 1962), p. 208.

46. Alistair Cooke, "Epitaph for a Tough Guy," *Atlantic,* May 1957, p. 31.

47. Philip Durham, *Down These Mean Streets a Man Must Go: Raymond Chandler's Knight* (Durham, N.C.: University of North Carolina Press, 1963), p. 69.

48. Citations to Chandler's *Farewell, My Lovely* are from the Ballantine reprint of the 1940 edition (New York, 1971).

49. Parker, p. 140.

50. Durham, *Mean Streets,* p. 128.

51. Gardiner, p. 232.

52. W. H. Auden, "The Guilty Vicarage," in *The Dyer's Hand and Other Essays* (New York: Knopf, 1956), p. 151.

53. Gardiner, pp. 214–15.

54. George P. Elliot, "Country Full of Blondes," *Nation,* April 23, 1960, p. 354.

55. Chandler, "Simple Art," p. 17.

56. Gardiner, p. 223.

57. Kenneth Millar, Introduction to *Kenneth Millar/Ross Macdonald: A Checklist,* ed. Matthew Bruccoli (Detroit: Gale Research, 1971), p. xvi.

58. Macdonald, p. 36.

59. Raymond Chandler, *The Big Sleep* (1939; rpt. New York: Ballantine, 1971), p. 47.

60. Raymond Chandler, *The High Window* (1942; rpt. New York: Ballantine, 1971), p. 19.

61. Chandler, *Farewell,* p. 121.

62. Durham, *Mean Streets,* pp. 3–4.

63. Durham, *Mean Streets,* p. 97.

64. Citations to Chandler's *The Big Sleep* are from the Ballantine reprint of the 1939 edition (New York, 1971).

65. Julian Symons, "The Case of Raymond Chandler," *New York Times Book Review,* December 23, 1973, p. 22.

66. Parker, p. 135.

67. Citations to Chandler's *The Lady in the Lake* are from the Ballantine reprint of the 1943 edition (New York, 1971).

68. Raymond Chandler, "Oscar Night in Hollywood," *Atlantic,* March 1948, p. 25.

69. Chandler, "Oscar Night," p. 24.

70. Citations to Chandler's *The Little Sister* are from the Ballantine reprint of the 1949 edition (New York, 1971).

71. Durham, *Mean Streets,* p. 5.

72. Ruhm, p. 177.

73. W. Somerset Maugham, "The Decline and Fall of the Detective Story," in *The Vagrant Mood* (Garden City, N.Y.: Doubleday, 1953), p. 126.

74. Mickey Spillane, in conversation, October 15, 1973.

75. Citations to Spillane's *I, the Jury* are from the New American Library reprint of the 1947 edition (New York, 1948).

76. Citations to Spillane's *One Lonely Night* are from the New American Library edition (New York, 1951).

77. Mickey Spillane, in conversation, October 15, 1973.

78. Citations to Spillane's *The Girl Hunters* are from the Dutton edition (New York, 1962).

79. Mickey Spillane, in conversation, October 15, 1973.

80. Quoted in Tom Shales, "Clint Eastwood: Strong, Silent and Very Rich," *Cincinnati Enquirer,* May 12, 1973, p. 30.

FOUR. The Far Side of the Brave New World

"It shakes you up when you've got a dead brunette in bed on your mind and then you get hit with a guy in a red velvet seat with a knife in him."

—Peter Chambers

An interesting exception to the role of the private eye as enforcer-savior is Ross Macdonald's Lew Archer, who "doesn't rush in there and save the values." [1] Macdonald, whose real name is Kenneth Millar, observed recently that what Archer does

> is a lot better than if the detective, in the name of virtue, goes around knocking people off. That, by many people, is taken as an indication of powerful virtue on the part of the character. The idea of knocking people off is just about the most powerful idea in modern American life. But I'm agin it. [2]

It has been Macdonald's feeling that "the detective-as-redeemer is a backward step in the direction of sentimental romance, and an oversimplified world of good guys and bad guys." [3] So Archer, surnamed after Sam Spade's partner in tribute to Hammett, finds empathy rather than rage the informing source for his actions. Like Spade and Marlowe, he is a solitary man without much money; but unlike them, his personal sense of guilt makes him more prone to pity than punishment. The reasons for his guilt are only hinted at in suggestions of past personal failure, incompletions of effort: he has lost his wife, he did not complete college, he resigned from the Long Beach force. Archer shares the southern California turf of Marlowe and Sam Spade, but not their unforgiving anger; his disappointment in the modern world has not yet made him give up on it. Confronted with a conscienceless adversary, it is possible for Archer to behave in a manner light years removed from Mickey Spillane: "I laughed in his face. I would have liked to have hit him. But there had to be a difference between the things that he might do and the things that were possible for me." [4] Instead of purging evil, Archer ministers to the little value he finds in a confined urban world where even the able are missing persons. "The hot breath of vengeance was growing cold in my nostrils as I grew older. I had more concern for a kind of economy in life that would help preserve the things that were worth preserving." [5] "He is vulnerable," writes Eudora Welty. "He cares." [6]

He had not always been so. Archer appeared first in *The Moving Target* (1949), a book that owed much to Chandler, and continued in several novels that were, in the estimation of John Leonard, "full of wisecracks and movie starlets, plutocrats and fisticuffs." [7] Then he was re-created in *The Galton Case* (1959), a book Macdonald has termed his "breakthrough novel." [8] Personal suffering led Macdonald to examine his own life and mine it for the materials of fiction. The writer had been born in California but was raised fatherless in Canada; his poor and depressed childhood became the source for a story about another displaced youth. Archer would serve as an intermediary to the truth; Macdonald explains that "a narrator had to be interposed, like protective lead, between me and the radioactive material." [9] *The Galton Case* is Ross Macdonald's departure from his antecedents and the beginning of the original and personal fiction he wrote later.

Archer is hired to find missing heir Tony Galton. The boy has been separated from his wealth and position since childhood; Archer shares his sense of dispossession. When he enters the well-appointed offices of a law firm in chapter 1, Archer notes they "convey the impression that after years of struggle you were rising effortlessly to your natural level, one of the chosen"; when he leaves, it is "like being expelled" (p. 3).[10] The boy's sense of expulsion is immediately Archer's own. The detective, who has "a reputation for tempering the wind to the shorn lamb" (p. 55), is like the boy an aristocrat without the trappings, brave and fine but poor. This is the source for their mutual vulnerability. Macdonald, in an essay on the novel, identifies the shared anguish of the sleuth in search of the boy in search of his father: "In a puritanical society the poor and fatherless, suffering the quiet punishments of despair, may see themselves as permanently and justifiably damned for crimes they can't remember having committed." [11] These "punishments of despair" only align Lew Archer and Tony Galton to a wider society of dispossessed, the human race; for all of us are failed versions of what we might be, exiles from an Eden of possibility. Poet Chad Bolling joins Archer midway through the novel and stands on a hill looking down at the city. His sense of loss is our own: "We could build another Athens. I used to think we could do it in San Francisco, build a new city of man on the great hills. A city measured with forgiveness. Oh, well" (p. 55).

"I wrote about the far side of the brave new world," noted Macdonald later; [12] if that brave new world is more penalty than promise, it is Macdonald's point that the results are the fault of those who made it. In treating "the epic theme of a lost father" in *The Galton Case,* Macdonald demonstrates what happens to the offspring of those who make mistakes. The sins of the fathers *are* visited upon the sons, not as punishment for the past but as consequence of it. The dead lie between Tony Galton and his inheritance; all he gets is the money.

Archer's effort in *The Galton Case* and the novels that follow is to find meaning in all of this. If, as Robert Brown Parker asserts, "the problems with which he must deal are finally problems which result from the failure of the family," [13] Archer's role is not to affix responsibility but to restore it. Archer alone is aware of the meaning of the single bird who raises his voice at the window in the final chapter as a reminder "of a world which encloses and outlasts the merely human." [14]

In *The Underground Man* (1971), which sold fifty-four thousand hardcover copies in six months, Macdonald refines and enlarges his lost-father theme to cosmic proportions. The first notes he made on the novel were recorded in a red spiral notebook: "An ecological crime." [15] The results of human greed in this book surpass personal disaster as metaphor for man's escalating war on his environment. Macdonald, a member of the National Audubon Society and the Sierra Club, has long been aware of the suicidal side of technology, and his sense of man embattled by the elements he unleashes is made concrete in the raging Rattlesnake fire of *Underground Man.*

The novel begins with Archer feeding "his jays." Birds will become emblematic; desk clerk Joy Rawlins later points out the pelicans at Dunes Bay: "They can't have any more young ones, did you know that? Their bodies are poisoned with DDT, and it makes their eggs all break" (p. 179).[16] Archer observes of a youth gone awry that "he belonged to a generation whose elders had been poisoned, like the pelicans, with a kind of moral DDT that damaged the lives of their young" (p. 226). All the young of *Underground Man* are blighted by their rich parents who "could afford to live in the open outside the city, right up against nature" (p. 67). But the consequence of that proximity is holocaust; a murdered man drops a lighted cigarillo, and "sparks and embers were blowing down the canyon, plunging into the trees like bright exotic birds taking the place of the birds that had flown" (p. 52). The destroying rich are never self-aware, nor do they accept any blame for what they have done. "We gave her everything," says one woman of her wayward daughter. "But it wasn't what she wanted" (p. 108).

The fire roars around and over the homes of the rich, who never understand what is happening to them. Smothering mothers hover over their lost progeny; Archer is in search of one woman's missing boy, while another, in the guise of shielding her hare-lipped, half-wit son, uses him as a shield between herself and the law. Still another hangs about uncertain and silent, "one of those waiting mothers who would sit forever beside the phone but didn't know what to say when it rang" (p. 102). Their poor stewardship stunts and twists what comes after them, leaving only a legacy of mistrust. Jean Broadhurst will not allow herself to rely on Archer:

> "You're quitting on me, aren't you?"
>   "No, I'm not."
>   "Do you want money, is that it?"
>   "It can wait."
>   "What do you want from me, then?"
>   "Nothing."
> She looked at me as if she knew better. People always wanted something. (p. 67)

Later Archer is confronted with the same doubt when he attempts to talk young Susan Crandall out of jumping from a bridge.

> "What will you do to me if I come back over there?"
> "Nothing."
> She said as if I hadn't spoken: "Shoot me? Or send me to prison?"
>   "Neither of those things."
>   "What would you do?" she repeated.
>   "Take you to a safer place."

She shook her head gravely. "There is no safe place in this world."

"A safer place, I said."

"And what will you do to me there?"

"Nothing."

"You're a dirty filthy liar!" (p. 210)

"I felt," Archer muses at one point, "as if we were going against nature" (p. 35), which is exactly the case.

The mercy that Archer extends out of an awareness of his complicity in the universe seems to be shared only by the least culpable, like Joy Rawlins, who feeds the frightened Ronnie Broadhurst the way Archer feeds his birds. Or like the solitary black man Archer encounters drinking cheap wine in the front seat of a car at dusk: "He put a mouth organ to his lips again and played a few bars of wheezy music. I'm guilty, it seemed to say, but I've suffered enough—so have you" (p. 77). Certainly this kind of compassion is missing from a man like land developer Brian Kilpatrick, who sees the young as "punishing us for bringing them into the world" (p. 84). Archer silently attends a scene illustrative of the moral abdication of the rich when Kilpatrick responds to a night caller at his home as the fire crawls down the mountain.

A rather wild-eyed young man with soot on his forehead was waiting at the front door.

Kilpatrick showed him the gun. "Get out of here. I don't have to put up with this kind of nonsense."

"You call it nonsense, do you?" the young man said. "I lost my house and my furniture. My family's clothes. Everything. And I'm holding you responsible, Mr. Kilpatrick."

"How am I responsible?"

"I talked to a fireman after my house burned down—too bad he wasn't there when it burned, but he wasn't—and he said that canyon should never have been built in, with the high fire hazard. You never even mentioned that when you sold it to me."

"It's a risk we all run," Kilpatrick said. "I could be burned out tonight or tomorrow myself."

"I hope you are. I hope your house burns down."

"Is that what you came here to tell me?"

"Not exactly." The young man sounded a little ashamed. "But I've got no place to spend the night."

"You're not going to spend it here."

"No. I realize that."

He ran out of words. With a parting look at the gun in Kilpatrick's hand, he walked quickly to a station wagon which was parked beside my taxicab. A number of children peered out through the back windows of the wagon, like prisoners wondering where they might be taken next. A woman sat in the front seat, looking straight ahead.

I said to Kilpatrick: "I'm glad you didn't shoot him." (pp. 90–91)

The aftermath of the fire will be worse than its onset: without trees to fasten the earth, the ground shifts, and Kilpatrick ends with several tons of symbolic soil blooped across his patio. Later he shoots himself in the game room of his doomed rich man's home. Archer, by contrast, gathers in the lost son of a murdered father and grandfather and ends sleeping protectively across the doorway to Ronnie's room.

Raymond Sokolov wrote that "Archer's leather-lined compassion for the small abducted boy is an implicit plea for human values in a society whose central metaphor may be the freeway with its constant movement, noise, pollution, brutality and lack of human control." [17] Control is what sets Archer apart from the damaged members of that society who, for Robert Brown Parker, "are in breathless pursuit of the American dream." [18] He is not innocent; William Patrick Kenny has observed rightly that "no one is innocent in Macdonald's novels." [19] But he is able as is no one else to accept the knowledge that every insignificant act has its sure consequence. The seismic tremors of human trespass may take generations to make themselves felt in the novels of Ross Macdonald, but at long last they bring whole dynasties down.

Macdonald has experienced fires like the Rattlesnake in his native Santa Barbara, where he lives with his wife, novelist Margaret Millar (*Beast in View*, 1955; *Beyond This Point Are Monsters*, 1970), and their dog Brandy, to whom Macdonald refers irreverently as "Lew." Like Archer, that conserver of values and men, Macdonald is an environmentalist, and it is not surprising that the cataclysmic California oil spill of 1969 found its way into his fiction. Natural disaster reaches mythic proportions in *Sleeping Beauty* (1973), a novel of wounded birds and wounded men.

Floating oil is the tangible ooze of a moral mire in the novel. The natural disaster has been occasioned by men; Macdonald's opening image is one of malign human intervention:

> [The spill] lay on the blue water off Pacific Point in a free-form slick that seemed miles wide and many miles long. An offshore oil platform stood up out of its windward end like the metal handle of a dagger that had stabbed the world and made it spill black blood. (p. 3) [20]

"You'd think it was the end of the bloody world," scoffs one of the corporation people responsible (p. 25), and indeed the once-white beaches take on the look of some primordial or postnuclear devastation: oil-blackened surfers sit hunkered before fires on shore "as if the end had come and they would never move again" (p. 4). The smear spreads with the tide and stains the cliffside windows of the Lennox family, whose oil dynasty has culminated in contagion. "Money is the glue that holds us all together," explains heiress Marian Lennox. "Money and oil" (p. 64). Like the oil, money is a source for power and contamination.

As Archer encounters young Laurel Russo (*née* Lennox) walking the oil-soaked sand, she stoops to lift a blackened grebe from the surf.

> I asked her what she was going to do with the grebe.
> "Take it home and clean it."
> "It probably won't survive, I'm afraid."
> "No, but maybe I will." (p. 4)

Laurel is a sustainer, as Archer is, but he later associates her with the dying bird: "I guessed that she had been badly hurt already, perhaps damaged like the grebe beyond hope of recovery" (p. 14). Both creatures are victims to an amoral industry, as is Laurel's murderess mother Marian, whose "graying hair, cut in a long shag, curled like wispy feathers at the nape of her neck. Her shoulder blades stuck out under her dress like unfledged wings" (p. 156). Archer will discover another oil-drowned grebe on Marian's patio before she steps quietly over the rail to her own death, and the sea-washed bodies of Nelson Bagley and Tony Lashman both bear black oil in the eyes and mouth. A reporter who wryly asks Archer if he is investigating the crime of pollution makes no connection between the dark ooze moving on the margins of the coast and the social slime that started it, but we do. Archer catches himself wishing "that we could live like the birds and move through nature without hurting it or ourselves" (p. 121), then sets out in pursuit of a lost Laurel among the orders of the weak and broken.

Laurel's father and mother, who "have spent practically their whole lives waiting to inherit" (p. 35), and her uncle, whose bad judgment set on the final stages of the spill and destroyed a naval craft the same way years before, are examples of the consequences of unexamined life; Laurel's grandfather, whose drive and vision created an empire, winds up a failing and destroyed man as a result of his long service to unprincipled profit. When Archer asks after the stricken millionaire, his doctor responds:

"Mr. Lennox is dead." His strained blue eyes came up to my face. "He was dead before I got to him. He was driving a bulldozer down the beach, and he had a heart attack."

"What was he doing on a bulldozer?"

"Trying to get rid of the oil, apparently." (p. 256)

The oil man's end is a self-parodying response to personal guilt; like Fitzgerald's careless people, William Lennox has never been one to clean up after himself. Archer finds a letter to Laurel in a book called *Permanent Errors;* the title spells out the finality of familial neglect.

Unlike the Lennoxes, who can attribute the oil spill to an act of God or even the conspiracy of an environmentalist, Archer accepts responsibility for Laurel, who has stolen his sleeping pills and left behind evidence of suicidal intentions. If company man Ben Somerville seems "to be an unreal man even when saying true things" (p. 230), if blackmailer Harold Sherry is victim to an angry dream and empire-builder William Lennox to an ambitious one, Archer keeps firm rein on his own fantasy, refusing to romanticize himself out of a difficult world:

Traffic was still fairly light, and the day was clear enough to see the mountains rising in the east like the boundaries of an undiscovered country. I lapsed for a while into my freeway daydream: I was mobile and unencumbered, young enough to go where I had never been and clever enough to do new things when I got there.

The fantasy snapped in my face when I got to Santa Monica. It was just another part of the megalopolis which stretched from San Diego to Ventura, and I was a citizen of the endless city. (pp. 84–85)

At one point in the story, Archer's eye is caught by an out-of-state car. "A sticker on the rear bumper of the Cadillac read, 'Honk if you love Jesus.' The children's dark eyes looked out at me in solemn question. Was this the promised land?" (pp. 236–37). It used to be, but things happened. Archer's understanding of those things make him the authentic figure to press his lips to Laurel's forehead at the end; like the persistent fairy-tale prince, his kiss will be the one to wake her—but to reality, not to romance.

Ross Macdonald is a moralist, which places him in the mainstream of private eye fiction, but his moralism is compassionate rather than vengeful, and his protagonist protects the innocent in place of punishing the guilty. Like the others of his fictive profession, Lew Archer travels territory where no one can be trusted or believed; unlike them, the fact makes him more sad than bitter. What results is a series of "novels of character about people with ghosts," as William Goldman expresses it,[21] novels that do not exorcise guilt but offer a means of dealing with it. Or as Macdonald himself expresses it: "Now that we've gone to the moon successfully, we have to explore the craters of the earth."[22] Archer's explorations have been recorded in fourteen languages.

But Macdonald's "benevolent hunter"[23] remains an exception. If, as Macdonald has reflected, "the 'hard-boiled' detective novel was invented to reflect American society,"[24] attention must be paid to the more prevalent and less compassionate versions of his competitors. Private eye writers set out to reveal the changing face of urban culture by what their heroes observed traveling through it. Perhaps unintentionally, more was revealed about that culture in what their heroes did than what they saw. For the tacit acceptance of these writers was that since matters were askew in America, it was a man's duty to adjust them. The courts were worse than useless, and the cops were corrupt when they were not stupid, so if a man wanted justice he would have to arrange for it himself. It did not matter that injustices might be committed in the pursuit of justice—the bystander was part of the problem. What mattered was that the knocks were distributed to those who deserved them.

The key to Archer is self-knowledge; the key to his colleagues is the lack of it. A man may commit murder to get a murderer and not be a murderer. It is the interesting argument for capital punishment. Abortively prohibited by the Supreme Court in 1972, the death penalty at this writing has already been restored by nineteen states. Its lingering popularity is curiously American. Thomas Thompson wrote of this phenomenon:

> Behind the talk of protecting policemen from killers, behind the pleas that there must be death to deal with the most gruesome of killers, behind all this is a dark place in the American character. A legal execution is among the most vicarious of experiences, a shiver for the collective spines. . . . I came to wonder why a government would give a man whatever he wanted to eat in his last hours, then burn and shock and destroy his tissues before they were nourished.[25]

Archer knows *he* is guilty; the prototypical private eye knows everybody else is. His job is to get them. The phrase that recurs on the lips of supporting players in these stories and their commentators alike is "He gets results." Best-selling mystery writers like Brett Halliday, John Evans, Henry Kane, Richard S. Prather, Stephen Marlowe, Ernest Tidyman, and genre-newcomer James Jones take the private eye novel from the forties well into the seventies with a constant vision: the law can't help, but somebody with a gun can. It is an admission that human events have gone beyond societal control and only an armed messiah will serve. Their books form a chronology of American moral disaster perhaps less shrill than Spillane but just as disturbing.

Brett Halliday (pseudonym of Davis Dresser), heavily influenced by the Hammett of *Maltese Falcon*, has been writing books about red-haired Miami detective Mike Shayne for thirty-five years. Shayne, who dates back far enough to have been played on television by Richard Denning and on film by Lloyd Nolan, survives in more than half a hundred Halliday titles and his own monthly magazine, the last of the old-style pulps. Distinguished chiefly by his hot temper and a fondness for Martel five-star cognac, Shayne's bent for third-person retribution manifests itself early—in *Dividend on Death* (1939), the first published Shayne story.

After Sam Spade's allegiance to ritual, Shayne's ceremonious brandy drinking and breakfast making receive lengthy treatment, as does his procedure for making perfect dripolator coffee. Like Spade, he looks rough; unlike Spade, there is evidence of a dear boy underneath. "When he smiled," writes Halliday, "the harshness went out of his face and he didn't look at all like a hard-boiled private detective who had come to the top the tough way" (p. 5).[26] Shayne shares the unsentimental Spade's insensitivity for passion: "I'm never sure that I know what a person means when he speaks of love," growls the redhead (p. 4), but that does not prevent a soupçon of emotional goo from emerging in his response to his nineteen-year-old blonde client.

Phyllis Brighton comes to Shayne with a peculiar problem. "They say I've got an Electra complex," she explains, "and it's driving me insane with jealousy because mother married Mr. Brighton and I'll kill her before I'll let him have her" (p. 7). Then she attempts to throw herself from Shayne's office window: "What's the use of . . . going on?" Shayne holds her back, for "he would have felt an instinctive repulsion if it were true, and she was not repellent." Later she offers herself to Shayne to "find out about myself." Shayne has pause to reflect that "nothing like this had ever happened to him before" (p. 51). Manfully refusing her handsome offer, unsoiled Shayne announces "*I'm* making myself responsible for you" (p. 12) and proceeds to perform less morally doubtful services, like suppression of evidence and conspiracy to murder.

Encountering the murdered mother and Phyllis at home in a bloody nightgown with a dripping butcher knife at hand, Shayne does the logical thing: he removes the nightgown and knife. "Something stunk about the entire set-up," writes Halliday. "He didn't know just what" (p. 26). But Shayne's instincts are vindicated as the girl's Electra complex is revealed to be the plot of psychiatrist Joel Pedique, who encourages insanity to see if Freud's theories work in reverse. "The individual must be sacrificed on the altar of scientific achievement" (p. 166), Pedique notes, wandering on-stage by accident on his way to another genre. Pedique is sexually ambiguous, as many of the "sinister" villains of the more macho private eye fiction tend to be; as such he is a man whom Shayne "would have instantly disliked if he had met him with no previous knowledge of him at all." Halliday's ensuing description approaches caricature:

> He was small-boned and dark-skinned. His black hair was too long and it glistened with oil, combed straight back from a V where it grew low on his forehead. His lips were full and unpleasantly red. His eyes were beady and nervous, and his nostrils flared as he breathed. (p. 13)

Pedique is also possessed of "plump hips," a "mincing" gait, and "effeminate hands." *A la* Joel Cairo, he is clearly not to be trusted.

Stock figures, too, are the gangsters of *Dividend on Death*. "Racketeer" Ray Gordon and his pasty-faced henchman Dick (who bears more than a little resemblance to Hammett's Wilmer) perform typically as follows:

> Gordon slapped him with his open palm again. Shayne slumped back against the wall. Murderous rage flamed in his eyes and his left hand was clenched into a fist but he couldn't disregard the covering Luger and the twitching lips of Dick. (p. 186)

It is not the only punishment Shayne absorbs in the progress of the case, which becomes complicated by other deaths and a missing masterpiece by Raphael. "You're so strong!" chirps Phyllis admiringly (p. 73), and well she might: after sundry beatings and two .45 slugs in the shoulder, a smashed collar bone and other wounds, by evening "with the exception of a painfully stiff right side Shayne felt pretty good" (p. 14). The next day he breaks down a door, though with the other shoulder.

The police seem familiar, represented by stolid Will Gentry,

head of the Miami detective bureau, and Peter Painter, chief of
the Miami Beach division. Gentry, who likes Mike, has the sense
to allow him free rein, knowing he will hand over all the answers
in good time, but picky old Peter expresses such persistent doubts
he winds up having to pay Shayne $500 out of his pocket for the
credit for breaking the case. Plus a $2000 reward. This is no
longer standard police procedure in Miami Beach. But credit is
all Painter gets, for the culprits are all dead by the time he arrives;
Shayne has arranged for them to bump each other off. "Justifiable
homicide," Shayne explains cheerfully. "Save the state plenty of
money" (p. 229). In a later novel Shayne marries Phyllis, who
subsequently dies in childbirth, leaving him to the attentions of
secretary Lucy Hamilton, who appreciates him more than Painter
does.

Mike Shayne qualifies as a hero because his motives, in spite of
his insistence otherwise, are really altruistic. He's a nice man who
only swings on other men with fewer scruples. He says he is unsentimental, but his vision of feminine innocence is straight out
of the Victorian sensibility. And it is precisely his sentimentality
and his scruples that get him into trouble; in the service of an
ideal, anything goes. Like the Frankenstein's monster of film,
Shayne is an ugly mug with a squishy-soft heart whose destruc-
tiveness is always a function of his good intentions. In the series of
sequels to the movie original, Frankenstein's exploits are a series
of disastrously oafish odysseys in the service of Love that culminate
in broken bodies and inadvertent injuries. It is the pattern of the
private eye, who is accepted as a hero in spite of the consequences
of his heroism. Paul Pine, even more un-self-aware than Shayne,
will in the progress of his passage from front cover to back contrive
to do away with not only his lady's adversaries, but at length the
lady as well when she disappoints him; the bride of Frankenstein
recoiled with good reason.

Ex-credit manager and pulp editor Howard Browne, writing
as "John Evans," created Chicago sleuth Pine in *Halo in Blood*
(1946). Pine, late of the State's Attorney's Office, has a dent in his
nose from high school football and a matching dent in his legal
sensibilities. Hired by plug-ugly millionaire John Sandmark
("You could have hung a lantern on his chin, but not without his
permission" [p. 11]) [27] to discourage Sandmark's stepdaughter from

marriage, he becomes romantically involved with the lady: "this
could become the one thing every man wants and which a few
men actually find" (p. 119). Leona responds by discovering the
usual soft center under Pine's hard (if broken) nosed shell:

> "You've got a hard finish," she said slowly, not smiling now.
> "But I don't believe you are quite so hard underneath it.
> Perhaps that finish is there because you've seen too much of
> the wrong side of people. You go in for crisp speech and a com-
> plete lack of emotion. In a way you're playing a part . . .
> and it's not always an attractive part. Yet there's plenty of
> strength to you, and a kind of hard-bitten code of ethics. A
> woman could find a lot of things in you that no other man
> could give her." (p. 96)

That "code" again; Nemesis was never so attractive. Leona turns
out to be one of the killers. The other is police lieutenant George
Zarr of the Homicide Detail, whom we didn't suspect all along.
Pine is implacable. He turns in Zarr—"You got a date with the
fireless cooker" (p. 151)—but his most dread anger is reserved for
the false Leona. Tending to her is not a vocational duty but a
personal one.

> "Murder is a matter between you and the State, baby. But
> when you try to lock the door permanently by running a love
> affair with me, selling me on how much you love me and I
> love you, laying me open for a kick in the teeth even bigger
> than the one I was just getting over—that is where it becomes
> a personal matter—a matter between you and me." (p. 165)

"You're finished, baby," Pine decrees. "You're all washed up.
You're done for." As in the Spade/O'Shaughnessy confrontation,
this meeting will mean curtains for the lady and annunciation for
the eye. The final page records the result of Pine's interrogation
and his conviction that it is good:

> "Oh, my dearest, haven't I suffered enough? I love you,
> Paul. I love you! Don't do this terrible thing to me!"
> I drew back my arm and brought the back of my hand

down across her face with all my strength. The blow knocked her away from me, drove her into a huddled heap on the floor. I said, "Before five this afternoon, you hear me? Either you tell it or I do."

She lay there, staring up at me. I turned and went into the reception hall, opened the door and closed it behind me.

The elevator was somewhere below. I put my finger on the button.

It was very quiet there in the small corridor. The only sound was the faint whine of the ascending cage. It came up slowly—too slowly for me. Yet I could wait. I knew how to wait. I could wait forever.

I was opening the elevator door when the sound came from behind the closed door to 6A.

It was a single sound. A sharp, brittle sound. The sound of a Colt .32. . . .

I got into the cage and rode down to the first floor and went out into the hot clean light of a new day. (p. 168)

Leona's induced suicide is Pine's prescription for "the hot clean light of a new day," and his reenactment of a continuing climax in private eye fiction underscores not only the peculiar ethic of the Op but a real hatred of women ancillary to it. The conception of woman as somehow impure and therefore dangerous—traceable by primitive societies to the menstrual cycle—is updated in a Puritan vision of the female as source of evil, demon lover in disguise. From Hammett's redhead to Spillane's "real blonde," the love interest in the American detective novel is often a fair-seeming witch who must be sought out and destroyed in the style of Salem. If she is not always demonstrably burned alive, as is the murderess at the end of Spillane's *Kiss Me, Deadly* (1954), she is unarguably terminated, freeing the again celibate eye to return to a secretary who, as domestic principle, is always unthreatening and always dull. The bullet in Leona Sandmark's brain is an American exorcism typical of the genre.

In *Armchair in Hell* (1948) Henry Kane's Peter Chambers, the wacky New York gumshoe once wounded in the buttocks at the Battle of the Bulge, sums up his story and that of his confreres like this:

> "Now there's an American private eye who has no wife, or sleep, or food, or rest. He drinks, drinks more, and more; flirts with women, blondes mostly, who talk hard but act soft, then he drinks more, then, somewhere in the middle, he gets dreadfully beaten about, then he drinks more, then he says a few dirty words, then he stumbles around, punch-drunk-like, but he is very smart and he adds up a lot of two's and two's, and then the case gets solved." (p. 45) [28]

At least so it goes in *Armchair*, which sports some of the most interesting thugs in fiction—including Chambers. There is the Little Guy, for example, who runs "a juicy bistro uptown," and gambler Viggy (for *vigorisch*) O'Shea, who summons the detective to his apartment for advice on what to do about the three dead bodies in it. Get rid of them, Chambers suggests wisely. And there is Crying-Towel Reed.

> Once upon a time, when Cry worked exclusively for the Little Guy, trouble developed with the slot machines. The cashboxes were sullied with a profusion of slugs. But regularly. So Crying-Towel Reed was given the assignment and he had a peephole drilled in the wall and an eye applied to the peephole and soon enough it was discovered that a chef in the joint who cooked for the customers had found a system to beat the bandits. When business was dull, he shoved slugs into the machine until he hit, then he quit till business was dull again, then he tried the system on another machine. They laid him down on the floor of the kitchen and they held him down by the arms and they held him down by the legs, and Cry injected quarters, not slugs, into his throat, unclinkingly, until he died. (p. 67)

No more slugs in the slot machines. And so Crying-Towel Reed purges the system of one of its liabilities. Interestingly enough, hero Peter Chambers performs the same way. When the oafish but aptly named Max Crumb beats the detective up, Chambers shoots him three times and breaks his back with a haymaker. "A private richard," Chambers confides, "must not absorb a licking unless he returns it twofold, approximately . . ." (p. 117). By the end of the case Chambers has matters so arranged that the Little Guy blasts killer Denny O'Shea (brother to Viggy) after Chambers's partner shoots Crying-Towel Reed, in payment for O'Shea's knifing of art patron Algernon Hale and cutting-up of go-between Charlie Batesem and exotic dancer Mona Crawford. "It happened exactly the way I wanted it to happen," intones the deadpan Chambers (p. 248).

The novels of Richard S. Prather (*Slab Happy*, 1958; *Dig That Crazy Grave*, 1961) concerning "happy-go-lookie" Los Angeles detective Shell Scott sold well in the millions, and Stephen Marlowe's stories of Washington operative Chet Drum (*Trouble Is My Name*, 1957; *Killers Are My Meat*, 1957) also enjoyed a wide audience. Both writers published paperback originals concurrently under the Fawcett Gold Medal label. Inevitably someone hit on the idea of a collaboration; the result was *Double in Trouble* (1959),[29] containing Scott, Drum, and twice the bodies and blondes of standard fare.

Scott becomes embroiled in the affairs of the Los Angeles local of the National Brotherhood of Truckers ("emphasis not so much on the brother, as on the hood" [p. 34]) when a friend of his is murdered after stealing evidence against the leadership. At the same time Drum is hired in Washington by the Hartsell Committee to look into the affairs of the union's headquarters there. White-haired ex-marine Scott ("my favorite hangouts are women" [p. 1]) finds himself crossing trails with crew-cut, Magnum-packing Drum, and they spend most of the novel waiting to take a swing at each other.

The opportunity affords itself at a tidewater Maryland airfield where each has tracked his faction. An internal war in the Union has resulted in Happy Jack Ragen's L.A. outfit, soldiered by heavies Roe Mink and "handsome death" Candello, jockeying for power against the Washington mob of Mike Sand and minions Glasses and Rover, sneakily refereed by power-hungry loan shark Abacus Abbamonte. While they gather for a wary midnight meeting, Scott and Drum slug it out on the tarmac outside. After refashioning each other's faces at some length, the two come to the belated conclusion that they have been on the same side all along. They pause to consider how best to deal with the opposition. "I'm afraid the only way we could take these gangs of hoodlums would be if they all cooperated by shooting themselves," says Scott, and the cowboys are off again.

> He looked at me strangely. That was about the only way he could look at anybody now, but I thought I detected a different strangeness. He said, "Scott, didn't you say we could take them if they'd shoot themselves?"
>
> "Yeah, but I'm likely to say anything. . . ."
>
> Then it hit me. And the indecision was suddenly over—for both of us. It was funny how we clicked then, as though the process of trying to murder each other had somehow welded us closer together than we could ever have been without it, as if during the blows and bloodspilling there had come about a kind of mental alchemy which let us think almost as one. (p. 249)

So the detectives engage in an infernal "brother-hood" of their own, blazing away at both factions to set them against each other. Scott is paying off Ragen's crew for the murder of his friend; Drum is evening the score for the kidnapping of his Lady by Sand's people. Their efforts meet with some success. Drum observes:

> It was bedlam. Astounding, amazing, unbelievable bedlam. But I believed it. Next to me a man jerked suddenly and blood splashed from his body onto my hand. He let out a high, soft sound and fell. Somebody screamed inside, really screamed, a man's voice but high and shrill. He didn't stop screaming; the voice just got weaker, softer. (p. 258)

Says Scott:

> Ragen had surrounded himself with thugs whose first impulse on hearing a gun go off was to yank out a heater and blast away. So he was getting no more than he'd asked for, a kind of crazy justice. . . . (p. 268)

"Crazy" seems to be the precise word as the terrible twosome close in on the objects of their most particular wrath. Scott seizes Ragen in a manner reminiscent of Mike Hammer's ungentle meetings with people he doesn't like on lonely bridges:

> I felt my fingers dig in, sinking into the flesh, felt rubbing of bone, slide of muscle. His hands wrapped around my wrists. I held him, choked him. A kind of craziness settled in my brain, craziness and ugliness. (p. 269)

Nor is Drum to be outdone as he confronts the goon who has been making marks on his girl:

> I said, "How are things in Front Royal, Lindzey?"
> He let go of Hope and sprang to his feet, hands empty. This was the part I would have to live with later, this was the part that would bother me. But he had done that to Hope. Kill him in cold blood? No, not in cold blood. He had done that to Hope.
> I shot him as he reached for his gun. (p. 264)

Double in Trouble is the formula all over again, multiplying the massacre to a suitable size for two. Scott and Drum battle each other and the bad guys with success, but they never fight free of the plot. Hammett wrote it as *Red Harvest* thirty years earlier.

Screenwriter Ernest Tidyman created the first black private eye in *Shaft* (1971), but the only new thing about the book is the hero's race. A cover blurb proclaims "Shaft has no prejudices. He'll kill anyone—black or white," placing him solidly in the private eye tradition. Shaft is a Vietnam veteran who has survived his slum youth, but not without resentment. He vents it periodically: when a Mafia button man spits at him, Shaft smashes a bottle of Scotch across his face; when a black hoodlum threatens him, he hurls him from his office window. (The office is four floors up.) But the height of Shaft's resentment is reserved for Vic Anderozzi, lieutenant of police.

Anderozzi's most offensive failing seems to be a weakness for hot cashews, but he is a cop, and Shaft cannot afford to be reasonable with him. "I have to know what's going on," Anderozzi objects aggrievedly (p. 14).[30] And while Shaft is giving him nothing, Anderozzi doggedly adjusts the evidence to cover for him and engages in exchanges like the following down at the 17th Precinct:

> "Why don't you bring him in for questioning?" the Commissioner suggested.
> "No," said Anderozzi. "He's doing better this way. Whatever he's doing." (p. 135)

Anderozzi is surely the most quiescent cop since S. S. Van Dine's Sergeant Heath.

Shaft's awareness of his body has a touch of the narcissist in it. He is always taking it to the gym or putting it through pushups because "he knew its value" (p. 37); consequently it responds with the astounding recuperative powers native to this kind of fiction, enabling him to scale buildings and do battle even with four cracked ribs and the usual collection of abrasions. It serves him well in other arts than the martial ones, and Shaft can actually ruminate on the uses to which his women might be put: "The floor was gritty. He wondered if he could work out some scheme with the chicks who woke up there [in his rooms] to clean up part of the place before they left" (p. 146). But Shaft's awareness does not extend to his mind.

> That's the way he was. Circumstance and response. Cause and effect were almost like Siamese twins of his nature, closer together than a couple of Harlem tenements. There was no room there for thought, reflection or perspective. The ball of his anger bounced from one hard wall to the other before there was time. Later, it made him wonder if he had not made a mistake. But it would be *much* later, *months* later. And there would be no guilt or self-doubt with his questions, for he was not questioning himself or his actions. Only the results. . . . (p. 131)

Thus when Shaft conceives insult by the mob, he seeks immediate redress. The result, inevitably, is holocaust. But the road there is not without a few grins. This is Shaft in search of the enemy:

" 'Hey, man,' Shaft said, leaning both hands on the brim of the bar, neither raising or lowering his voice but speaking slowly and clearly, 'where the hell is the headquarters of the Mafia?' " (p. 154). After talking with a soldier for the Organization in (where else?) the Cafe Borgia, Shaft receives the once-a-book wages of the private eye: a thorough beating.

His mission is to rescue the kidnapped daughter of Harlem hoodlum Knocks Persons; the Mafia wants to trade her for the heroin trade in Harlem. This would mean, for reasons that are unclear, civil war; so Shaft, armed with his anger and a team of black revolutionaries, sets out to get the girl back. "I'm going to burn down Thompson Street," announces the black detective (p. 191). "It was," notes Tidyman later, "a small price to pay for the whole of Harlem" (p. 198).

Burn down Thompson Street he does. Scaring the citizenry to hysteria with a mock riot, Shaft pursues them maniacally. "He waved them on with the .45. They fell past him in blind panic, hysteria. When they were two flights below him, part of a fighting, struggling mass to get out of the building, he fired two more shots into the air" (p. 208). The diversion is successful, and after a gun battle Shaft returns to the street with the rescued girl over his shoulder. Here is the scene that greets him:

> There was a body in the street. No, two. He looked up Thompson and saw a car moving through the mass, pushing people aside with its fenders and bumpers. A fat man in a bathrobe didn't get out of the way in time. The car went over his leg and he screamed, then rolled into the mass around him. (p. 210)

The car is driven of course by Shaft's wheelman. When it is over and the black detective reflects on the carnage behind him, he has no difficulty justifying any of it: "The four men who died on Thompson Street were the worst, the very worst of men, police records down to the floor, killers every one of them. Kidnappers, drug peddlers. . . . They happened to die while a licensed agent was performing a service for a client" (pp. 213–14). No mention is made of the injured innocents and the damage done to their homes, but it was, again, a small price to pay for the whole of

Harlem. And will there be an accounting with the law? Not as long as there is an Anderozzi to reassure the commissioner.

"What went on with the grand jury today?"
He snorted.
"Not much," he said. "They decided I wasn't a murderer. They came out with something they call a no bill. Prosecutor chewed on me hard." He paused to think of the district attorney's anger. "But what the hell, I been chewed on before, will be again. Just reminded me what the rules are about being a detective. Said I violated about a hundred seventy-seven laws."
"What laws?"
"Well, there's a lot of gun laws, for one thing. Then there's some shooting laws. And then there's some killing laws. And some setting-fires laws. All kinds of laws. It figured out to be about one hundred seventy-seven I broke. Technically."
"Are you in trouble?"
"No." (p. 213)

The Tidyman film script for *Shaft* omits the riot, gaining the girl by other means; presumably the American movie audience is unprepared for images of Shaft running amok to the cry of "The niggers are coming!" Such squeamishness does not extend to shots of the black man sailing his foes from windows. Or shooting them in the head. Shaft can bawl out black guerrilla Ben Buford for getting his friends killed with a revolutionist's idealism and attack kingpin Knocks Persons for exploiting his people for money, but really Shaft is guilty himself of both failures in awareness: he readily indulges in public mayhem with the blithe conviction that he is serving the cause of human liberation (Harlem's in general and the black girl's in particular), and he hands Persons back his daughter and his empire for $20,000, having made the world safe for the black pusher. Shaft's conception of himself as a hang-loose hero has to be mystifying to anyone whose name is not Anderozzi.

"I'm not a pig," asserts global Op Lobo Davies discriminately. "I'm more what you'd call a wart hog, I guess. Or a werewolf" (p.

59).[31] Davies is the invention of war novelist James Jones (*From Here to Eternity*, 1951; *The Thin Red Line*, 1964), a late entrant to the private eye field with the recent *A Touch of Danger* (1973). Davies, working for an inflationary $150 a day and expenses, is a "graduate lawyer" who carries a flathead sap in his briefcase and puffs his lips in and out when he thinks, like Nero Wolfe. His lips are in little danger of wear, for Davies's cerebrations confine themselves to variations of "I was glad I was a private eye and not a hippie" (p. 194) or "[old age] was a problem everybody had to face, if he lived long enough" (p. 233). "I was not one of those men who at almost fifty had to hold in their stomach and breathe shallow," smirks Davies, flexing (p. 131), for he is nothing if not physical: Davies's idea of "fun" is to hit people in the face with his forehead, which he does repeatedly and with all the self-congratulatory relish of Colonel Cantwell's aging confrontations in *Across the River and into the Trees*.

Jones's debts to Hemingway practically place the novel into receivership. One of them is his hero's belief in blueprints for behavior: "The only code I had ever found that worked was that as long as you worked for him and took his money, the client was right, or if you didn't like what he wanted you to do, you didn't take the job" (p. 35). An example of Davies's application of this code is his assignment by one employer to collect a debt. Davies evidently finds the job properly inoffensive and accepts it. "There was no question I was working for the right side," he explains piously. Here's how the graduate lawyer applies himself to his task:

> I hadn't talked much. There wasn't much point. I had just made my points, carefully. Without any warning I hit him. Then I proceeded methodically to beat him up. As he probably expected me to. I didn't honestly know what he expected. That I would go away and leave him alone, maybe. But he knew the underworld rules as well as I did. (p. 38)

The "underworld rules," whatever those are, evidently receive some support from the occupationally punctilious Davies. But there's more:

> I could go on beating him up forever, he pointed out.
> He was almost eloquent.
> I nodded grimly. "Quite true. And I may. Do you have any children?" (p. 38)

Then the graduate lawyer proceeds "methodically" to break one of the debtor's fingers. He comes up with the money. "I would do it again if I had to," signs off Davies (p. 40), leaving us with that warm feeling that comes from watching sincere dedication at work.

Davies becomes involved with a blackmailed countess and the headless body of a drug trafficker, but when young surf sprite sweet Marie is murdered with an outboard motor some of Davies's habitual composure flakes away. "I suppose this has become a vendetta for you now; hasn't it?" queries the breathless countess. "It sure has," rumbles Davies unsurprisingly (p. 286). Another Davies rule is "I always pay what I think I owe" (p. 88), an economy that looks forward and backward in the plot.

It seems Davies had a partner once (appropriately or not named Watson), just "another Wasp from Denver in the Heartland." The partner ends up "shot dead by a doped-up Negro gunman on South State Street in Chicago" (p. 290). What Davies does about it is not unexpected.

> I found him because I had close friends on the South Side.
> . . . I probably could have saved his life. For about thirty seconds during our discussions he'd been about ready to give it up and turn himself over; if I'd asked him. I didn't ask him. Instead, I let him think he'd fooled me into trusting him. I did it, deliberately. So he went on sweet-mouthing me, with his slippery mean eyes. Until he thought he could get the drop on me, like he had my partner. When he went for the gun he had hidden in the back of his belt, I was all ready and waiting. (p. 293)

No more Negro. Jones has done his homework; he has read the other private eye writers and borrowed them blind of everything except Lobo's description, which of course bears a close resemblance to Jones himself. But many of these writers deal with idealized versions of themselves who deal actively with evils their lot is only to identify. (Ex-detective Hammett, whose overweight Op bore no physical relationship to his tubercularly gaunt creator, is a notable exception.) Their heroes will receive ritual beatings that entitle them to retaliate. As Lobo Davies confides at one point, "I felt like Wyatt Earp, walking down the dusty main drag of Tombstone looking for a showdown with somebody" (p. 184). The irony is unintentional; recent studies suggest Earp was a road agent and the gunfight at the O.K. Corral only another execution.[32]

The innocent in American literature is justly celebrated as an emblem for the essential and well-intentioned virtue of democratic man. He comes to learn something of the corruption loose in the world by perceiving an inkling of it inside him; he then purifies himself in a symbolic act of rejection. Huck Finn finds some of the landsman's insensitivity in himself and chooses Hell, freeing himself and Jim. Christopher Newman acknowledges the intriguer's temptation in himself and burns the papers that could confirm it. Nick Carraway regrets his own careless romanticism and arranges the funeral of his friend. Huck's last promise is to "light out for the territory"; Newman is bound back for America; and Carraway leaves the East for keeps.

The private eye novel has been perceived by some to be another manifestation of this enduring American theme. The eye *is* an innocent, honest, unsparing of his efforts, who learns of earthly villainy by moving within it. But the suggestive thing is that he does not learn of corruption through self-awareness, and his consequent acts are not directed toward his own purification, but everybody else's. He is entitled to mete out justice because he is *already* pure; and so his performance entangles him in evil rather than liberating him from it. Mike Shayne gets people killed; so do Paul Pine and Peter Chambers and Shell Scott and the whole combat-ready crew. Pains are taken to suggest that the people they kill always somehow deserve it; but were there any insight on the part of these characters that in pursuit of murderers they have themselves become murderers, surely the logical ending of these stories would entail a punitive blowing-off of the eye's own angry head. For the eye is the American innocent gone mad. His search for truth is only an inventory of slaughtered scapegoats that teaches him nothing. At the end he begins no symbolic journey to a better place, having sent too many others there before him.

NOTES

1. Quoted in Jon Carroll, "Ross Macdonald in Raw California," *Esquire*, June 1972, p. 149.

2. Carroll, pp. 149, 188.

3. Ross Macdonald [Kenneth Millar], "The Writer as Detective Hero," *Show*, January 1965, p. 36.

4. Ross Macdonald, *Sleeping Beauty* (New York: Knopf, 1973), p. 250.

5. Ross Macdonald, *The Underground Man* (New York: Knopf, 1971), p. 253.

6. Eudora Welty, review of *The Underground Man*, by Ross Macdonald, *New York Times Book Review*, February 14, 1971, p. 29.

7. John Leonard, "Ross Macdonald, His Lew Archer and Other Secret Selves," *New York Times Book Review*, June 1, 1969, p. 19.

8. Ross Macdonald [Kenneth Millar], Foreword to *Archer at Large* (New York: Knopf, 1970), p. ix.

9. Ross Macdonald, Foreword to *Archer in Hollywood* (New York: Knopf, 1967), p. vii.

10. Citations to Macdonald's *The Galton Case* are from *Archer at Large* (New York: Knopf, 1970), pp. 1–192.

11. Ross Macdonald [Kenneth Millar], "A Preface to *The Galton Case*," in *Afterwords: Novelists on Their Novels*, ed. Thomas McCormack (New York: Harper and Row, 1969), p. 152.

12. Kenneth Millar, Introduction to *Kenneth Millar/Ross Macdonald: A Checklist*, ed. Matthew Bruccoli (Detroit: Gale Research, 1971), p. xv.

13. Robert Brown Parker, "The Violent Hero, Wilderness Heritage and Urban Reality: A Study of the Private Eye in the Novels of Dashiell Hammett, Raymond Chandler and Ross Macdonald," Diss., Boston University, 1971, p. 147.

14. Macdonald, "Preface," p. 150.

15. Raymond A. Sokolov, "The Art of Murder," *Newsweek*, March 22, 1971, p. 102.

16. Subsequent citations to Macdonald's *The Underground Man* are from the Knopf edition (New York, 1971).

17. Sokolov, p. 102.

18. Parker, p. 150.

19. William Patrick Kenney, "The Dashiell Hammett Tradition and the Modern Detective Novel," Diss., University of Michigan, 1964, p. 144.

20. Subsequent citations to Macdonald's *Sleeping Beauty* are from the Knopf edition (New York, 1973).

21. William Goldman, "The Finest Detective Novels Ever Written in America," *New York Times Book Review*, June 1, 1969, p. 2.

22. Quoted in Sokolov, p. 108.

23. Quoted in Sam Gragg, Jr., "Ross Macdonald: At the Edge," *Journal of Popular Culture*, 7, No. 1 (Summer 1973), p. 219.

24. Quoted in Gragg, p. 214.

25. Thomas Thompson, "California Looks for a Better Way to Kill," *New Times*, January 25, 1974, p. 38.

26. Citations to Halliday's *Dividend on Death* are from the Henry Holt edition (New York, 1939).

27. Citations to Evans's *Halo in Blood* are from the Bantam reprint of the 1946 edition (New York, 1958).

28. Citations to Kane's *Armchair in Hell* are from the Simon and Schuster edition (New York, 1948).

29. Citations to Prather and Marlowe's *Double in Trouble* are from the Fawcett edition (Greenwich, Conn., 1959).

30. Citations to Tidyman's *Shaft* are from the Bantam reprint of the 1971 edition (New York, 1972).

31. Citations to Jones's *A Touch of Danger* are from the Doubleday edition (New York, 1973).

32. See Frank Waters, *The Earp Brothers of Tombstone: The Story of Mrs. Virgil Earp* (New York: C. N. Potter, 1960); and Ed Ellsworth Bartholomew, *Wyatt Earp 1879–1882: The Man and the Myth* (Toyahvale, Texas: Frontier, 1964).

FIVE. The Last of the Bloodshot Eyes

"I have a little system of my own. . . ."
—Charles Manson

The absolute reductio ad absurdum of the private eye novel would proceed much like a parody strip once drawn by Al Capp in mockery of Chester Gould's popular *Dick Tracy*. Capp called his hero Fearless Fosdick, a poorly paid but assiduous flatfoot, and set him on the trail of a poisoned can of beans. Fosdick's method of saving the populace from consuming that solitary contaminated tin was to shoot holes in everybody he discovered opening a can of beans. He ended in eating the poisoned can himself. Similarly, *Pogo* creator Walt Kelly's clever Spillane satire, "Gore Blimey" by "Mucky Spleen," resolves itself in the summary arrest of a hero who shoots out slow-changing traffic lights. These comic figures become victims to their own missionary zeal—as are all those unfortunates casually acquainted with them.

Even more outrageous caricatures are now being widely sold as serious inventions. The new private eye is an unemployed crypto-soldier with a grudge. Typically he has seen intimates murdered by the mob; his response is personal vendetta, the bloody consequences of which far outstrip those of the original transgressors. Traveling anonymously—like the Op on nobody's salary—the "hero" systematically seeks out the ungodly and mows them down, city by city. Cases in point are Don Pendleton's "Executioner," Jon Messman's "Revenger," Peter McCurtin's "Avenger," Frank Scarpetta's "Marksman," Mickey Spillane's "Gill," Mike Barry's "Lone Wolf" (not to be confused with the urbane creation of Louis Joseph Vance), Al Conroy's "Soldato," and Richard Sapir and Warren Murphy's "Destroyer." Possessed like the Op of anonymous *nommes de guerre,* they achieve what identity they permit themselves through violence. The proliferation of these personalities and others like them demonstrate the national sense of impotence in dealing with organized crime. The law cannot do it; then other measures must be taken. But, curiously, the picture of governmental agencies in these stories comes increasingly close to the popular vision of the "Syndicate." Many of these murderous

135

social workers operate with the tacit acceptance, and even active support, of federal agencies. Admiring local cops help flame-eyed Mack Bolan. Ex-*mafioso* Johnny Morini picks off mobsters under the guidance of the Justice Department. And automaton-killer Remo Williams has been trained by the American government to kill in defense of its Constitution. Like Fosdick, these extraordinary creatures are instruments not for the establishment of justice but for the dissolution of due process. Unlike Fosdick, they are not funny. The accounts of their alarming adventures are fraught with serious dissertations on honor and patriotism in support of the slaughter, making the authors even more terrifying than their creations. Their arguments for duty in defense of mass murder are as familiar as the testimony at the trial of William Calley.

Both as philosophy and as art the stories are importantly flawed. Hitchcockian reticence, so necessary to establish the decorum for sustained emotional *frisson,* is altogether absent. The blood is belly-deep; walls are washed in it. Scarpetta's lighthearted "Marksman" is capable of lofting about unsocketed eyeballs in jest. So the recent spate of vengeance stories heralds an end to the private eye. The nature of his work is still morally sanctioned murder, but he has lost his profession; now he works for himself—or for the government—doing what he has always done without the distractions. No longer need he contend with incautious clients, interfering loyalties, uneven evidence. Nor with any ambiguities at all.

The trend for the seventies began with Don Pendleton's fell Mack Bolan novels, novels of such popularity that "Pendleton" (after the marine base?) produced sixteen of them in two years. They spring from a single premise. While Bolan was in the service overseas, his sister Cindy became indebted to a gangland loan shark. She sold herself to make the payments. Bolan's father found out about it and settled matters by shooting Cindy, his wife, and himself. So Bolan, returning home, vows to use his martial skills on the mob.

His buddies in Vietnam had called him "the Executioner" in tribute to his proficiency as a jungle fighter, infiltrator and sniper. He had become a specialist in "seek and destroy" missions of a personal nature, his nerveless efficiency and cool

contempt of death staying with him through numerous pene-
trations of hostile territories and accounting for more than
ninety official kills of enemy bigwigs during his two tours of
combat duty in Southeast Asia.

So now this government-trained war machine was on a
different kind of combat tour—but the ground-rules remained
the same. Seek out and destroy the enemy—one by one, two
by two or fifty by fifty, the numbers did not matter. The
important thing was to carry the war to the enemy, to put at
least some show of resistance to the creeping inroads of organized crime. They had evidently found the laws of a free
society particularly suited to their own manipulation—so
Bolan placed himself also above the restrictions of American
justice. "I am not their judge. I am their judgment. I am
their executioner." So saying, he set out to prove it and to
bring a taste of jungle hell to these enemies at home. (pp.
10–11) [1]

Each book records a fresh Bolan campaign in a separate city. He
blasts the badhats with everything in the arsenal from assault
machine guns to antitank weapons, then presses a marksman's
medal into the palms of his victims for signature. This is not to
suggest he is without sensitivity. An example of Bolan's finer
feelings occurs in *Vegas Vendetta* (1972) as he closes on the syndicate convoy he has just ambushed: "A guy was staggering out of
the target vehicle with his clothing in flames. Bolan took a step
forward then grimaced and quickly sent a mercy burst from the
Stoner into the human torch" (p. 20). As Pendleton makes clear,
"In Bolan's mind, this was the sole difference between himself
and his enemies. He was still a human being" (p. 37). He certainly
exhibits real fraternal attachment; when he encounters Vegas
entertainer and Bolan ally Tommy Anders backstage in the company of two unfamiliar Italians, Bolan inquires brusquely:

"Are these the boys that muscled you?"
"Yeah, that's them," the comic replied in a choked voice.
The Beretta whispered without preamble, another Para-
bellum found mortal flesh and bone, and both *mafiosi*
crumbled to the floor. (p. 64)

It is unfair for Anders to mourn that "the country is losing its guts" (p. 61), for vestiges of the old spirit remain strong in those who subscribe to the methods of the Executioner—such as the police. "I wouldn't have much faith in a world that wouldn't make room for a Mack Bolan," grits out one wounded cop, and we learn that although the "young crusader" has been a mass murderer in the eyes of the law, "many individual policemen were secretly sympathetic" (p. 12). Indeed, the evidence is that the FBI itself is "dragging its heels" (p. 38). And so Bolan, licensed by personal loss, will continue to remove the "rot" from the "American swing scene" (pp. 185–86) as long as Pendleton can keep up the pace.

Bolan is not alone. *The Revenger* (1973) by Jon Messman records what happens when the mob attempts to muscle store-owner Ben Martin: he pistol-whips one Mafia intermediary and jams a letter opener through the hand of another. Boss Joe Colardi interprets these acts as unfriendly ones and promptly kidnaps Martin's young son. In an unguarded moment the boy crawls off a tenement roof, and Martin arms for retribution. The police as usual remain aloof ("We've got nothing here" [p. 47]),[2] but Martin has his own resources, and blows the heads off at least eleven hoods. As the score piles up, a thoughtful Don Genosanti reflects that Martin is no ordinary mark:

> "He is not simply a small-time operator, nor merely a tough cookie. I called some connections in the right places and I got a line on this man. Mr. Ben Martin was a soldier in Vietnam, a special kind of soldier, one of maybe a half-dozen such men. He was a specialist."
>
> "What kind of a specialist?"
>
> "A specialist in assassination, in hand-picked targets always deep in enemy territory or in places where the job was hard to do. Not just killing, mind you, but assassination. The CIA and the Army Intelligence boys picked the targets, special generals, certain officials, sometimes even South Vietnam big shots who were causing trouble. Every target took a lot of care in getting to and even more in killing. But doing the job and getting away clean was maybe the most important of all, and that's what he was trained to do." (p. 95)

He is, in other words, a professional killer, like the men he is after. And like the men he is after he has Sicilian notions about "vengeance and honor and the payment of debts" (p. 114). He hopes to convey those notions to a timid America that has not yet learned that the only way to deal in justice is "to bear the shield and the sword":

> There would be payment for those who had made their dirty rottenness into an accepted part of society. And there would be a learning for all those who watched, for they would see that the creeping, crawling, slimy sickness could be stopped. But not by turning away, not by platitudes, not by weakness, but only by wrath, towering, consuming wrath that refused to live with wrong. (p. 78)

Martin, equipped with a personal grudge, is also equipped with the means to indulge it. Old Father Donatello told him once as a boy that each of us has a mission; Martin discovers his behind the eyepiece of a sniper scope.

Robert Briganti's wife and child are killed early in Peter McCurtin's *Manhattan Massacre* (1973), and their deaths become the loud report for yet another emotional stampede. The police again prove inadequate ("legally they had nothing to go on" [p. 30]),[3] so Briganti picks up an army M79 grenade launcher and a 9 mm. UZI submachine gun and stalks off after the ungodly, arguing the collusion of the United States government.

> The government could stop the Mafia, but there is too much money at stake. Every time a new Attorney General takes office they go through the same old ritual. A brand new anti-Mafia task force is organized, a new crime committee is convened and maybe a few top mobsters are called—and naturally they take the Fifth—and what else is new. Frank Costello lost his U.S. citizenship because he got it by fraud, and they still couldn't manage to get him out of the country. The Justice Department deported Carlos Marcello, but knowing the right people got him deported right back to the States. . . . (p. 191)

"If the law is powerless to stop these men, then I will," vows Briganti (p. 104), and stop them he does in an appropriately crimson fashion. But he seems at moments rather unparticular about the bystanders. Robbing a weapons warehouse, Briganti gives no pause to the prospect of casual killing:

> He went forward slowly, and now the Hi-Power was cocked and he knew he wouldn't hesitate to kill this workingman he didn't know. Not for a moment did he think about this unknown man's life: his wife, his kids (if he had a wife or kids), his fantasies, his fears. He had come only a short way, and he had a long way to go. (p. 43)

He has gone further than he knows. The crime that Briganti finds inconceivable is the routine murder of his family, but it seems only inconceivable for someone else. Not only are mobster Coraldi and company fair game, but anybody in the way as well.

> He didn't know what he would have done if the two cops in the patrol car had stopped to ask hard questions over the ends of cocked .38s. Well, yes, when he thought about it again he knew what he would have done. He would have killed both men before they even got close. He knew he could do it: it wouldn't take more than one shot apiece. It wasn't right, but it was right for him. . . . (pp. 34–35)

"They had something in common, he and Coraldi," thinks Briganti without irony (p. 181). His personal war gains national attention when he mails taped accounts of his doings to network newsmen and federal agents by way of heartening the populace in the fight against crime. Amazingly, the populace *is* heartened, but the FBI and CIA wind up fighting over whose agent they think he is, so close are his methods to their own.

Philip Magellan, the protagonist of Frank Scarpetta's *Mafia Wipe-Out* (1973), also has a wife and son to avenge, but his techniques are even less attractive than Briganti's. With typical inventiveness, Magellan decides to demoralize one especially vain foe with facial surgery:

Magellan ripped off Mario's jacket and used it to scoop up more broken shreds of glass lying around them. Then he shoved the jacket hard into Mario's face and held it there. He rubbed the jacket up and down. Mario screamed. He struggled to escape. Magellan wouldn't let go. When he finally released his victim, Mario's face was covered with blood and broken pieces of glass of all sizes embedded into his skin. It didn't look like a human face at all. (p. 48) [4]

And that is not all. Magellan is not only able to cut off an adversary's legs with a propeller, he can even use one of them to club down another attacker. At the end of the novel he seals the door to a basement room where he has arranged for a few Mafia men to be severally dismembered and boiled alive. But these exertions are for the good of society: "the very future of life on earth was at stake" (p. 60). As author Scarpetta is at pains to point out, "these were a strong and determined and clever group of nefarious criminals and if Philip Magellan were not at hand to put a stop to their deadly plans, who knows where it would all end up" (p. 87). Who knows, indeed. Meanwhile the police spend their time in the background arguing over whether or not the rumored existence of the Mafia is anti-Italian propaganda.

The police in Mickey Spillane's *The Last Cop Out* (1973) are equally befuddled. Someone has been bumping off high-ranking criminals all over the country, and instead of calling on semi-retired Mike Hammer they install suspended cop Gill Burke to find out who the culprit is. The Gill, as almost everybody in the novel admits, has been suspended "because he was too much cop for the politicians to live with" (p. 22); [5] he had been ready to bust the gangs wide open, but the fix was in. Mild Mr. Lederer, beleaguered district attorney, would rather handle matters without him, but Burke sees fit to lecture the lawyer on fine points:

"Mr. Lederer," Burke said, "those weren't murders."
"Oh?"
"They were killings."
"What's the difference?"
Burke's lips pulled tight across his teeth. "If you don't know, telling you won't make you understand at all." (p. 42)

The difference is of course that "killings" are justified, and it comes as no surprise to the reader that Burke has been behind them all along. "Screw the Miranda or the Escobedo decisions," snaps supercop Burke (p. 181), who sees his way clear once more to save the state money. Burke's depredations are so devastatingly effective some mobsters consider the possibility he is a federal man.

In Mike Barry's *Bay Prowler* (1973), Burt Wulff is not a federal man, but he feels that he is at least "working along with the police" (p. 60).[6] Wulff's gripe is the loss of a girl friend, which he views as cause enough for a personal assault on the drug trade. One thing that particularly irritates Wulff is the enemy's capacity for cold-blooded killing. Confronting Trotto, a young syndicate killer, Wulff offers a homily on the evils of impersonal violence:

> "Don't kill me. Don't kill me!"
> "I have to," he said. "You see, the trouble is, Trotto, that you just don't care. You just did your job always, you never thought about what it meant or what was happening to people. People never meant anything to you, Trotto; you never thought about them. But if you're going to be a piece of machinery then you have to pay the price of being machinery. When it malfunctions, you replace it."
> He raised the gun.
> "It's nothing personal," Wulff said as the man started to run, and shot him. (p. 69)

If the end of the argument seems to take some of the force from Wulff's side, the reader is reminded that Wulff is a "good man" (p. 48) whose war "was for the victims" (p. 26). Like the cops slowly wising up, Wulff adheres to new rules. He lives in troubled times. Even the lawmen are loading for the end:

> They wanted more than the regulation equipment which the cities were issuing them. Walking around the inner cities all day was enough to convince you that a pistol would never be enough. They wanted full riot gear, they wanted a battery of devices, they wanted mace and tear gas and even deadlier stuff, and they wanted to have access to them at all times. . . .
> There was a new breed coming in at the edges which invented

their own code or more likely none at all. They would do anything to get their share of the power.

So the country, underground, was turning into an arsenal.
It might not take the fabled enemy attack at San Francisco to
blow this city up, much less the famous earthquake that was
supposed to be due at any time at all, next year by the latest.
Most likely when the city went up it would be the enforcers,
those sworn to protect it from attack, who would do the blowing. Imagined attack and then the overreaction. The base-
ments would empty and the blood would be running fresh
and free in the streets. (pp. 137–38)

"Everything was falling apart" (p. 130) muses Wulff; he sees the
Organization as a corporate structure the evils of which are the
evils of any big business in America. Kingpin Frank Severo is "a
good American" after all (p. 79), ailing from an American disease:
junk, the narcotic variety, correlative of junk, the bureaucratic
kind. But Wulff is emphatically not a businessman himself. When
Severo suggests he is merely trying to get a job done the same
way the *capo* is, Wulff is quick to correct him: "It isn't a job. . . .
It's a pleasure" (p. 112). And he shoots him, bringing the country
that much closer to a cleaner, nonbureaucratic tomorrow.

"You'll get sub rosa thanks from the Justice Department for
this, Johnny," says a federal liaison man to Johnny Morini for
similar efforts in Al Conroy's 1973 *Murder Mission* (p. 192).[7]
Johnny has his objections to organized crime as the others do, but
his exertions are underwritten and endorsed by the government.
Unofficially. "We want Don Marno," Morini is informed at the
book's beginning—"along with anyone else of importance you can
pick up along the way" (p. 25). Johnny, an ex-Mafia soldier, is
now on the other side, but his tactics are reminiscent of the past.
To ingratiate himself with the coveted Don Marno he arranges
for the gang leader's nephew to be pushed between a pier and a
yacht that could easily crush the child so he can mimic a rescue.
Others he does not rescue. Morini kidnaps a lawyer, blows up a
boat. Strangles somebody. Still, whatever it is Morini does, "he
had been doing it in the line of duty" (p. 79). The liaison man
will offer his departmental absolution: "You're doing a job that
your country thanks you for . . ." (p. 115).

As is Remo Williams, angry hero of Richard Sapir and Warren Murphy's *Murder's Shield* (1973). Williams is "the killer arm for an agency set up outside the U.S. Constitution to preserve that Constitution from organized crime, revolutionaries, and from all who would overthrow the nation" (p. 39).[8] Set on the track of an organization of off-duty police officers using their spare time to eliminate unprosecutables ("We say no to the vicious and the depraved who prowl our streets" [p. 79]), Williams encounters a serious moral dilemma: he agrees with the opposition. "I'm going against the good guys," groans Williams (p. 38).

> Out there in the city were thousands of criminals, thousands who would rob and hurt and maim and kill. Thousands, of whom only a fraction were ever caught and punished by the law. What made it so wrong if the police helped the law along? It was only what Remo himself did. (p. 164)

"They're doing our job," Williams protests (p. 55), and never have hero and villain attained such a conscious identity in the entire genre. Williams manages to overcome his qualms long enough to go ahead with his murders, but clearly the whole affair does not sit well with him. The arguments offered up to him seem somehow unconvincing.

> "Remo," said Smith, his voice tense and low, "your function parallels what these people are doing, so you see them as doing right. But there are differences. One, we use you only in dire emergencies when we have no alternative. Two, we exist precisely to prevent the sort of thing that is going on now. CURE exists so America won't become a police state. We were commissioned so this wouldn't happen." (pp. 55–56)

Even on a second reading, the logic here seems elusive.

These stories, far less artfully written than the ones that came before them, detail the final degeneration of a peculiarly American figure once conceived to be a hero. Somewhere he changed sides; as his moralism became more and more besieged by an underworld no longer contained by an urban context, he came

to see himself as an infiltrator traveling incognito in enemy territory—the globe. Vidocq's counter-police and Pinkerton's bomb
raid on Castle James have come full circle; the Mafia and the federal government are two sides of the same coin for the wild purist
who views himself as the last clear hope on earth for justice. Suddenly the private eye is beyond even Spillane's Oscar Deamer;
now the names of those he resembles closest call to mind other
true believers with strange visions of new and equitable worlds:
Oswald, Ray, Sirhan, Bremer.

At one juncture in his trial for the Sharon Tate killings, Charles
Manson crawled across the defense table and screamed at the
judge: "In the name of Christian justice, someone should cut your
head off!" [9] He might have been Mike Hammer. The evangelism
of violence has become an American institution; these novels only
reflect the trend bound out beyond fiction. As the law becomes
increasingly unable to deal with burgeoning American crime (and
Manson was held responsible for killings subsequent to the Tate
matter), increasingly irrational solutions have been brought to
bear; as the criminal goes mad, so do his pursuers. We become
witness to a grim gyre of lawbreaking lawmen: first Chandler's
Maglashan sees illegal procedure as the necessary method for in-
suring conviction; then the same writer's DeGarmo falls victim
of a transitional schizophrenic killer-cop duality; until at last John
Evans's George Zarr loses himself utterly to the other side. So the
"good" cop leaves the force in disgust—to become another Maglashan. In 1973 Don Siegal's "Dirty Harry" Callaghan finishes out
his first film by throwing away his badge, and John Sturges's more
recent *McQ* (John Wayne unhorsed) will begin his exploits with
the same unambiguous gesture. Movies like *The French Connection* and *Serpico* deal with increasingly disaffiliated police officers
who, in their impatience with a massively corrupt and inefficient
system, become essentially institutional private eyes, cowboys in
blue whose uniforms are their only link to more corporate law
enforcement. Indeed, the fictive private eye is frequently a cop
who called it quits. Even Eddie Egan, ex-vice squad prototype for
plainclothes film narc "Popeye" Doyle, has opened a detective
agency of his own. Life imitates art. And the novelist's answer to
the Knapp Commission and Patrick Gray's *Doorbell Rang* FBI
remains the private eye, society's collective exorcist, a battered

professional who builds a wall of booze between his damaged
sensibilities and the world and who carries out a policy that supports the harrowing and terrible conclusion of Alan Harrington:
"the best way to deal with psychopaths and outlaws is to become
more like them." [10] And so in the service of God the private eye
becomes God, Jonathan Edwards's angry answered prayer.

The infamous White House "Plumber's Unit" has demon-
strated how deeply this notion of hard measures has insinuated
itself into American institutions. The official defense of the legion
of lapsed lawyers involved in the illegalities of Watergate has been
that they conducted their euphemistically dubbed "dirty tricks"
not for money but for the good of the country—making Remo
Williams something more than a pulp artist's pipe dream. Rumors
have already been passed, however founded or unfounded, that
the Plumbers could credibly have been involved in the taking off
of George Wallace—*pro bono publico*. The men testifying at
Watergate hearings were not the wild-haired demons of motor-
cycle sagas but scrubbed, crew-cut Haldemans, bright, bifocaled
Deans, men whose very purity of purpose revealed the ragged
outer edge of American rectitude, the edge Melville saw in the
whiteness of the Whale. CIA agent E. Howard Hunt, himself a
writer of thrillers, began living out his fantasies of dangerous men
in the service of an ideal—and helped save his country from the
awful uncertainty of making its own political choices, while G.
Gordon Liddy shot out light bulbs for the ladies and a besieged
Edmund Muskie burst into tears in a symbolic New Hampshire
snow. The incredible story of the private eye is the simplified
story of self-destructive American moralism—agents of MRA doing
larceny and murder for everybody's good, mercy bursts for the
masses.

And in an era of iron gates and guard dogs the private eye still
holds an audience among those who would seek a messiah with a
gun. For he is no longer wish fulfillment for a frustrated nation
but the emblem of American rage, the archangel Michael making
war in Hell. Peter Gay has written of him—or of someone like him
—wisely and well:

> the justification for anarchism is the anarchist's confidence
> that his own judgment is superior to the constituted process

within which change legitimately occurs. This is to put violence in the place of persuasion, elitism in the place of debate, the cynical exploitation of legal technicalities in the place of authentic respect for a system of order—in a word, it is to put will in the place of reason. Those who despise form *know* that they are right; like Robespierre, they are pure, and being pure, they are dangerous.[11]

"Most likely when the city went up it would be the enforcers, those sworn to protect it from attack who would do the blowing"; the time cries out for heroes, but not this kind. For America looks out through a Pinkerton orb like the divine eye on the dollar, and Lew Archer is a lonely man.

NOTES

1. Citations to Pendleton's *Vegas Vendetta* are from the Pinnacle edition (New York, 1972).
2. Citations to Messman's *The Revenger* are from the New American Library edition (New York, 1973).
3. Citations to McCurtin's *Manhattan Massacre* are from the Dell edition (New York, 1973).
4. Citations to Scarpetta's *Mafia Wipe-Out* are from the Belmont Tower edition (New York, 1973).
5. Citations to Spillane's *The Last Cop Out* are from the Dutton edition (New York, 1973).
6. Citations to Barry's *Bay Prowler* are from the Berkley edition (New York, 1973).
7. Citations to Conroy's *Murder Mission* are from the Lancer edition (New York, 1973).
8. Citations to Sapir and Murphy's *Murder's Shield* are from the Pinnacle edition (New York, 1973).
9. Alan Harrington, *Psychopaths* (New York: Simon and Schuster, 1972), p. 44.
10. Harrington, p. 137.
11. Peter Gay, "Law, Order, and Enlightenment," in *Is Law Dead?*, ed. Eugene V. Rostow (New York: Simon and Schuster, 1971), p. 31.

List of Works Cited

Abrahamsen, David. *Our Violent Society*. New York: Funk and Wagnalls, 1970.

Anon. "Nick Carter and the Professor; or, Solving a Scientific Problem." *Nick Carter, Detective: The Adventures of Fiction's Most Celebrated Detective*. New York: Dell, 1963, pp. 268–320.

Anon. "The Silver Age: Crime Fiction from Its Heyday Until Now." *Times Literary Supplement*, February 25, 1955, p. xi.

Auden, W. H. "The Guilty Vicarage." *The Dyer's Hand and Other Essays*. New York: Knopf, 1956, pp. 146–58.

Baring-Gould, William S. *Nero Wolfe of West Thirty-Fifth Street*. New York: Viking Press, 1969.

———. *Sherlock Holmes of Baker Street: The Life of the World's First Consulting Detective*. New York: Clarkson N. Potter, 1962.

———. "Two Doctors and a Detective: Sir Arthur Conan Doyle, John H. Watson, M.D., and Mr. Sherlock Holmes of Baker Street." *The Annotated Sherlock Holmes*. 2 vols. New York: Clarkson N. Potter, 1967. I, 1–109.

Barry, Mike. *Bay Prowler*. New York: Berkley, 1973.

Bartholomew, Ed Ellsworth. *Wyatt Earp 1879–1882: The Man and the Myth*. Toyahvale, Tex.: Frontier, 1964.

Blake, Nicholas [C. Day-Lewis]. Introduction to *Murder for Pleasure: The Life and Times of the Detective Story*. Howard Haycraft. London: Peter Davies, 1942, pp. xv–xxvii.

Brown, Richard Maxwell. "The American Vigilante Tradition." *Violence in America: Historical and Comparative Perspectives; A Report to the National Commission on the Causes and Prevention of Violence, June 1969*. Ed. Hugh Davis Graham and Ted Robert Gurr. New York: New American Library, 1969, pp. 144–93.

Carroll, Jon. "Ross Macdonald in Raw California." *Esquire*, LXVII: 6 (June 1972), 148–49, 188.

Cawelti, John G. *The Six-Gun Mystique*. Bowling Green, Ohio: Bowling Green University Popular Press, 1973.

149

————. "The Spillane Phenomenon." *Journal of Popular Culture,* III:1 (Summer 1969), 9–22.

Chandler, Raymond. *The Big Sleep.* 1939; rpt. New York: Ballantine, 1971.

————. *Farewell, My Lovely.* 1940; rpt. New York: Ballantine, 1971.

————. *The High Window.* 1942; rpt. New York: Ballantine, 1971.

————. *The Lady in the Lake.* 1943; rpt. New York: Ballantine, 1971.

————. *The Little Sister.* 1949; rpt. New York: Ballantine, 1971.

————. "Oscar Night in Hollywood." *Atlantic,* March 1948, pp. 24–27.

————. "The Simple Art of Murder." *The Simple Art of Murder.* 1939; rpt. New York: Ballantine, 1972, pp. 1–22.

Chesterton, G. K. "The Divine Detective." *A Miscellany of Men.* New York: Dodd, Mead, 1912, pp. 277–83.

————. "How to Write a Detective Story." *The Spice of Life and Other Essays.* Ed. Dorothy Collins. Beaconsfield, England: Darwin Finlayson, 1964, pp. 15–21.

Clurman, Robert. Introduction to *Nick Carter, Detective: The Adventures of Fiction's Most Celebrated Detective.* New York: Dell, 1963, pp. 7–14.

Conroy, Al. *Murder Mission.* New York: Lancer, 1973.

Cooke, Alistair. "Epitaph for a Tough Guy." *Atlantic,* May 1957, pp. 31–35.

Cooper, James Fenimore. *The Last of the Mohicans.* 1826; rpt. New York: Scribner's, 1961.

Cuthbert, Norma B., ed. *Lincoln and the Baltimore Plot 1861: From Pinkerton Records and Related Papers.* San Marino, Calif.: Huntington Library, 1949.

Dey, Frederick. "Nick Carter, Detective." *Nick Carter, Detective: The Adventures of Fiction's Most Celebrated Detective.* New York: Dell, pp. 15–68.

Doyle, Arthur Conan. *The Complete Sherlock Holmes.* Garden City, New York: Doubleday, Doran, 1930.

Durham, Philip. "The Black Mask School." *Tough Guy Writers of the Thirties.* Ed. David Madden. Carbondale and Edwardsville: Southern Illinois University Press, 1968, pp. 51–79.

————. *Down These Mean Streets a Man Must Go: Raymond Chandler's Knight.* Durham, N.C.: University of North Carolina Press, 1963.

Edenbaum, Robert I. "The Poetics of the Private Eye: The Novels of Dashiell Hammett." *Tough Guy Writers of the Thirties.* Ed. David Madden. Carbondale and Edwardsville: Southern Illinois University Press, 1968, pp. 80–103.

Elliot, George P. "Country Full of Blondes." *Nation,* April 23, 1960, pp. 354–60.

Ephron, Nora. "Lillian Hellman Walking, Talking, Cooking, Writing, Walking." *New York Times Book Review,* September 23, 1973, pp. 2, 51.

Evans, John [Howard Browne]. *Halo in Blood.* 1946; rpt. New York: Bantam, 1958.

Fiedler, Leslie. *Love and Death in the American Novel.* New York: Criterion, 1960.

Fitzgerald, F. Scott. *The Great Gatsby.* New York: Scribner's, 1925.

Frantz, Joe B. "The Frontier Tradition: An Invitation to Violence." *Violence in America: Historical and Comparative Perspectives; A Report to the National Commission on the Causes and Prevention of Violence, June 1969.* Ed. Hugh Davis Graham and Ted Robert Gurr. New York: New American Library, 1969, pp. 119–43.

Gardiner, Dorothy and Katherine Sorley Walker, eds. *Raymond Chandler Speaking.* Freeport, N.Y.: Books for Libraries Press, 1962.

Gardner, Erle Stanley. "Getting Away with Murder." *Atlantic,* January 1965, pp. 72–75.

Gay, Peter. "Law, Order, and Enlightenment." *Is Law Dead?* Ed. Eugene V. Rostow. New York: Simon and Schuster, 1971, pp. 21–31.

Goldman, William. "The Finest Detective Novels Ever Written in America." *New York Times Book Review,* June 1, 1969, pp. 1–2.

Goulart, Ron. Introduction to *The Hardboiled Dicks: An Anthology of Pulp Detective Fiction.* Los Angeles: Sherbourne Press, 1965, pp. xi–xviii.

Gragg, Sam Jr. "Ross Macdonald: At the Edge." *Journal of Popular Culture* VII:1 (Summer 1973), pp. 213–22.

Gruber, Frank. *The Pulp Jungle.* Los Angeles: Sherbourne Press, 1967.

Halliday, Brett [Davis Dresser]. *Dividend on Death.* New York: Henry Holt, 1939.

Hammett, Dashiell. *The Big Knockover: Selected Stories and Short Novels of Dashiell Hammett.* Ed. Lillian Hellman. New York: Vintage, 1972.

———. *Blood Money.* Cleveland: World, 1943.

———. *The Maltese Falcon. The Novels of Dashiell Hammett.* New York: Knopf, 1965, pp. 293–440.

———. *Red Harvest. The Novels of Dashiell Hammett.* New York: Knopf, 1965, pp. 3–142.

———. "The Whosis Kid." *The Return of the Continental Op.* New York: Dell, 1945, pp. 10–71.

Harrington, Alan. *Psychopaths.* New York: Simon and Schuster, 1972.

Higgins, George V. "The Private Eye as Illegal Hero." *Esquire*, LXVIII:6 (December 1972), 348–51.

Hofstadter, Richard. "Reflections on Violence in the United States." *American Violence: A Documentary History*. New York: Knopf, 1971, pp. 3–43.

Horan, James D. *The Pinkertons: The Detective Dynasty That Made History*. New York: Crown, 1967.

Jones, Archie H. "Cops, Robbers, Heroes and Anti-Heroes: The American Need to Create." *Journal of Popular Culture*, I:2 (Fall 1967), 114–27.

Jones, James. *A Touch of Danger*. New York: Doubleday, 1973.

Kane, Henry. *Armchair in Hell*. New York: Simon and Schuster, 1948.

Kenney, William Patrick. "The Dashiell Hammett Tradition and the Modern Detective Novel." Diss., University of Michigan, 1964.

la Cour, Tage, and Harald Mogensen, eds. *The Murder Book*. New York: Herder and Herder, 1971.

LaFarge, Christopher. "Mickey Spillane and His Bloody Hammer." *Saturday Review*, November 6, 1954, pp. 11–12, 54–59.

Lawrence, D. H. "Fenimore Cooper's Leatherstocking Novels." *Studies in Classic American Literature*. 1923; rpt. Garden City, N.Y.: Doubleday, 1951, pp. 43–54.

Leonard, John. "Ross Macdonald, His Lew Archer and Other Secret Selves." *New York Times Book Review*, June 1, 1969, pp. 2, 19.

Lowndes, Robert A. W. "The Contributions of Edgar Allan Poe." *The Mystery Writer's Art*. Ed. Francis M. Nevins, Jr. Bowling Green, Ohio: Bowling Green University Popular Press, 1970, pp. 1–18.

Macdonald, Ross [Kenneth Millar]. Foreword to *Archer at Large*. New York: Knopf, 1970, pp. vii–xi.

———. Foreword to *Archer in Hollywood*. New York: Knopf, 1967, pp. vii–ix.

———. *The Galton Case*. *Archer at Large*. New York: Knopf, 1970, pp. 1–192.

———. "A Preface to *The Galton Case*." *Afterwords: Novelists on Their Novels*. Ed. Thomas McCormack. New York: Harper and Row, 1969, pp. 146–59.

———. *Sleeping Beauty*. New York: Knopf, 1973.

———. *The Underground Man*. New York: Knopf, 1971.

———. "The Writer as Detective Hero." *Show*, January 1965, pp. 34–36.

Malin, Irving. "Focus on 'The Maltese Falcon': The Metaphysical Falcon." *Tough Guy Writers of the Thirties*. Ed. David Madden. Carbondale and Edwardsville: Southern Illinois University Press, 1968, pp. 104–9.

Maugham, W. Somerset. "The Decline and Fall of the Detective Story." *The Vagrant Mood.* Garden City, N.Y.: Doubleday, 1953, pp. 101–32.

McCurtin, Peter. *Manhattan Massacre.* New York: Dell, 1973.

Messman, Jon. *The Revenger.* New York: New American Library, 1973.

Millar, Kenneth. Introduction to *Kenneth Millar/Ross Macdonald: A Checklist.* Ed. Matthew Bruccoli. Detroit: Gale Research, 1971, pp. xi–xvii.

Nolan, William F. *Dashiell Hammett: A Casebook.* Santa Barbara, Calif.: McNally and Loftin, 1969.

Nye, Russel. *The Unembarrassed Muse: The Popular Arts in America.* New York: Dial Press, 1970.

Parker, Robert Brown. "The Violent Hero, Wilderness Heritage and Urban Reality: A Study of the Private Eye in the Novels of Dashiell Hammett, Raymond Chandler and Ross Macdonald." Diss., Boston University, 1971.

Partridge, Ralph. "Detection and Thrillers." *New Statesman and Nation,* January 9, 1954, pp. 47–48.

Patai, Raphael. *Myth and Modern Man.* Englewood Cliffs, N.J.: Prentice-Hall, 1972.

Paterson, John. "A Cosmic View of the Private Eye." *Saturday Review,* August 22, 1953, pp. 7–8, 31–33.

Pendleton, Don. *Vegas Vendetta.* New York: Pinnacle, 1972.

Pinkerton, Allan. *The Expressman and the Detective.* Chicago: W. B. Keene, Cooke, 1875.

———. *History and Evidence of the Passage of Abraham Lincoln from Harrisburg, Pa., to Washington, D.C., on the Twenty-third of February, Eighteen hundred and sixty-one.* U.S.A.: n.d., n.p.

———. *The Model Town and the Detectives.* New York: G. W. Carleton, 1876.

———. *The Molly Maguires and the Detectives.* 1877; rpt. New York: G. W. Dillingham, 1905.

Poe, Edgar Allan. *The Complete Works of Edgar Allan Poe.* 17 vols. Ed. James A. Harrison. New York: AMS Press, 1965.

Post, Melville Davisson. "The Doomdorf Mystery." *101 Years' Entertainment: The Great Detective Stories 1841–1941.* Ed. Ellery Queen [Frederic Dannay and Manfred B. Lee]. New York: Little, Brown, 1941, pp. 262–74.

Prather, Richard S., and Stephen Marlowe. *Double in Trouble.* Greenwich, Conn.: Fawcett, 1959.

Rowan, Richard Wilmer. *The Pinkertons: A Detective Dynasty.* Boston: Little, Brown, 1931.

Ruhm, Herbert. "Raymond Chandler—From Bloomsbury to the Jungle—and Beyond." *Tough Guy Writers of the Thirties.* Ed. David Madden. Carbondale and Edwardsville: Southern Illinois University Press, 1968, pp. 171–85.

Sapir, Richard, and Warren Murphy. *Murder's Shield.* New York: Pinnacle, 1973.

Sayers, Dorothy, ed. *The Omnibus of Crime.* New York: Harcourt, Brace, 1929.

Scarpetta, Frank. *Mafia Wipe-Out.* New York: Belmont Tower, 1973.

Schaefer, Jack. *Shane.* Cambridge, Mass.: Riverside Press, 1949.

Seelye, John. "Buckskin and Ballistics: William Leggett and the American Detective Story." *Journal of Popular Culture,* I:1 (Summer 1967), 52–57.

Shales, Tom. "Clint Eastwood: Strong, Silent and Very Rich." *Cincinnati Enquirer,* May 12, 1973, p. 30.

Sokolov, Raymond A. "The Art of Murder." *Newsweek,* March 22, 1971, pp. 101–2, 104–6.

Spillane, Mickey. *The Girl Hunters.* New York: Dutton, 1962.

———. *I, the Jury.* 1947; rpt. New York: New American Library, 1948.

———. *The Last Cop Out.* New York: Dutton, 1973.

———. *One Lonely Night.* New York: New American Library, 1951.

Stead, John Philip. *Vidocq: A Biography.* New York: Ray Publishers, 1954.

Stout, Rex. "Booby Trap." *Not Quite Dead Enough.* New York: Farrar and Rinehart, 1942, pp. 109–220.

———. *The Doorbell Rang.* New York: Viking Press, 1965.

———. *Fer-de-Lance.* New York: Farrar and Rinehart, 1934.

———. "Not Quite Dead Enough." *Not Quite Dead Enough.* New York: Farrar and Rinehart, 1942, pp. 1–108.

Sturak, Thomas. "Horace McCoy, Captain Shaw, and the *Black Mask.*" *The Mystery and Detection Annual.* Ed. Donald K. Adams. Pasadena, Calif.: Castle Press, 1972, pp. 139–58.

Symons, Julian. "The Case of Raymond Chandler." *New York Times Book Review,* December 23, 1973, pp. 13, 22, 25, 27.

Thompson, George J. III. "The Problem of Moral Vision in Dashiell Hammett's Detective Novels." Diss., University of Connecticut, 1972.

Thompson, Thomas. "California Looks for a Better Way to Kill." *New Times,* January 25, 1974, pp. 38–41.

Tidyman, Ernest. *Shaft.* 1970; rpt. New York: Bantam, 1972.

Van Dine, S. S. [Willard Huntington Wright] *The Benson Murder Case.* New York: Scribner's, 1926.

———. *The Bishop Murder Case.* New York: Scribner's, 1929.

———. *The Greene Murder Case.* New York: Scribner's, 1927.

Vidocq, Eugène-François. *Vidocq: The Personal Memoirs of the First Great Detective.* Trans. and ed. Edwin Gile Rich. Cambridge, Mass.: Riverside Press, 1935.

Walsh, John. *Poe the Detective: The Curious Circumstances Behind "The Mystery of Marie Rogêt."* New Brunswick, N.J.: Rutgers University Press, 1968.

Waters, Frank. *The Earp Brothers of Tombstone: The Story of Mrs. Virgil Earp.* New York: C. N. Potter, 1960.

Welty, Eudora. Review of *The Underground Man,* by Ross Macdonald. *New York Times Book Review,* February 14, 1971, pp. 1, 28–30.

Wertham, Fredric. *The Show of Violence.* 1949; rpt. New York: Bantam, 1967.

Westlake, Donald E. *Cops and Robbers.* 1972; rpt. New York: New American Library, 1973.

Wilson, Edmund. "Who Cares Who Killed Roger Ackroyd?" *A Literary Chronicle: 1920–1950.* Garden City, N.Y.: Doubleday, 1956, pp. 338–45.

———. "Why Do People Read Detective Stories?" *A Literary Chronicle: 1920–1950.* Garden City, N.Y.: Doubleday, 1956, pp. 323–27.

Wright, Willard Huntington. "The Detective Story." *The Great Detective Stories: A Chronological Anthology.* New York: Scribner's, 1927, pp. 3–40.